the Labrador Retriever

A COMPREHENSIVE GUIDE TO
BUYING, OWNING AND TRAINING

BY STEVE SMITH

Willow Creek

For the Rocket

Text © 2000 Steve Smith

Photo Credits: **Denver Bryan**, pages 2, 7, 15, 16, 19, 22, 26, 38, 44, 73, 78, 79, 94, 95, 105; **Ron Kimball**, pages 4, 12, 74; **Randy Handwerger**, page 5; **Gary Kramer**, page 8; **Cheryl A. Ertelt**, pages 10, 11, 98, 106; **Elizabeth Flynn**, page 17; **Norvia Behling**, pages 14, 21, 33, 37, 39, 48, 57, 71, 75, 81, 83, 84, 85, 89, 91; **Tara Darling/DogInk**, pages 27, 34, 45, 46, 61, 62, 63, 64, 66, 65, 108; **Bonnie Nance**, pages 41, 55, 56; **Kent & Donna Dannen**, pages 53, 59, 76, 77; **Dale C. Spartas**, pages 100 (2 photos), 103. Copyrights for the photos belong to the photographers.

Published by Willow Creek Press, P.O. Box 147, Minocqua, Wisconsin 54548
Designed by Patricia Bickner Linder

Library of Congress Cataloging-in-Publication Data
　　Smith, Steve
　　　The Labrador retriever : a comprehensive guide to buying, owning and
　　training / by Steve Smith.
　　　　p. cm.　(Breed basics series)
　　　ISBN 1-57223-387-7
　　　1. Labrador retriever. I. Title. II. Series.
　　　SF429.L3　S538　2000
　　　636.752'7--dc21
　　　　　　　　　　　　　　　　　　00-009072

Printed in Canada

Contents

The Lab Personality

THERE ARE A NUMBER OF GOOD REASONS WHY THE Labrador retriever is America's, and perhaps the world's, most popular dog breed. While Labs certainly possess brains and brawn in equal part, the thing that has set the breed apart from other canines in the minds and hearts of Americans is the dog's personality. It is unique; it is delightful and endearing; and it's all Labrador retriever — 100 percent. Labs are kind, caring animals that want to please you. Look at a Lab as he or she watches you. The dog will make eye contact, reading you, trying to determine what it is that will please you. Want to play ball? Fetch the paper? Get down on the living room carpet and wrestle? If that's what you want, that's what we'll do, those eyes seem to say.

Those of the opinion that on the Seventh Day, God made the Labrador retriever notwithstanding, the reason for their personality is because of the way in which the breed was developed. The Labrador retriever's past, like that of many now-recognized breeds, is incomplete and a matter of some conjecture. Certainly there is evidence that a retriever of the type that eventually became the Lab was developed by English fishermen plying the waters off Newfoundland; the dogs were used to retrieve both the fish caught in nets and the nets as well. That the breed got its beginning in the British Isles is beyond question, and the first Labrador retriever was registered with the Kennel Club in 1903. In the States, the Lab is a johnny-come-lately; the breed was first recognized by the American Kennel Club (AKC) in the 1920s.

The retrieving breeds, and the Labrador in particular, owe their personalities to the dog's sporting heritage. The Lab is a gonzo hunter and retriever. But as a retriever, he cannot do the thing that his molecules tell him to do — retrieve downed waterfowl and gamebirds — until the sportsman has done his thing. So, unlike the pointing breeds and hounds that hunt quasi-independently of their handlers, the Lab needs his or her person. The bond thus historically and genetically struck, the dog cannot vary from the devotion he feels for his human helpmate. Anyone who has ever felt the great, warm weight of a devoted dog against his or her leg — the "Labrador Lean" — knows that this bond is total, complete, and lifelong.

Labrador retrievers are friendly dogs, non-threatening (although protective) with humans and other animals. They make great watchdogs because of their wonderful senses, but their friendliness leaves them wanting in the guard dog department, which is just fine with most people.

They are among the leaders in lending a helping hand wherever they can. They excel as guide dogs for the seeing impaired, as search and rescue dogs, and as therapy dogs visiting shut-ins.

Training your Lab is fun, for both of you. The dogs love to work and please you, and this translates into ease of getting your point across. These animals do not respond well to heavy-handedness, but instead thrive on praise. However, give it sparingly — they are not fawning animals, and a constant "good boy" or "good girl" tends to cloud the issue

Labrador retrievers love to please their owners, and they thrive on praise.

at hand. Instead, a stroke of the head or pat on the flank is usually sufficient to show them you approve of what they are doing.

THE LAB, LIKE ALL CANINES, has three separate, distinct phases of life: puppyhood, adulthood, and old age. Some animal behaviorists note that all pet dogs remain puppies throughout their lives because they are dependent on someone else (you) for their food, much as wolf pups depend on a parent to bring home food to the den. That's why, these folks say, dogs greet us at the door at the end of the day in the same manner wolf pups greet Mom and Dad. Well, I'm not sure about that. I like to believe my Labs love me and can't wait to see me, and I'll bet you feel the same way about yours.

Even if you never plan to compete, hunt, or trial, training your dog is an imperative. He is going to have to take his place in your world, and the Lab's size and fun-loving ways make disciplined training essential — or else you'll have an untamed juggernaut to contend with for the next dozen or so years. The basic commands of *heel, come,*

The best thing you can do for your Lab is to wear him out every day of his life.

sit, *stay* and *down* will cover just about everything you'll need to make your pup into a good citizen, one that is able to take its place in human company.

PUPPYHOOD, WHICH THIS BOOK explains, is the time for rapid growth and quick learning. The pup's young brain, like that of all mammals, is growing and absorbing experiences, regulations, and your family's traditions, and he or she will test you in much the way children test parents. All the basic rules and obedience commands should be taught at this time, within the first year, and properly within the first six months. (Can you teach an old dog new tricks? Sure. Is it easy? No.) Pups are adventurous, inquisitive, and hyperactive. They need a controlled, loving environment lest they harm themselves, fall prey to accident, or grow up to be undisciplined hooligans.

In his adult years, the Lab is a faithful companion with an unquenchable desire for work and activity. Dogs from about three through eight, though well trained, need activity lest they figure out ways to entertain themselves — and they will. Some dogs never seem to outgrow their puppiness — my five-year-old dog Roxie the Rocket greets me at the door each night when I come home from work with not one but two tennis balls stuffed in her mouth, waiting to have me toss her some fetches. When I tire of the game, Rox takes her tennis balls to a stairway in the house and bounces them down the steps, watching from the top until they are halfway down, then charging after them as they carom across the family room on the lower level. She will give herself fetches this way for hours, or until I holler at her to knock off the noise.

Well-trained, adult Labs are among the smartest dogs, ranking fourth on the canine intelligence testing scale. But this intelligence, along with their active nature, can get them into trouble on occasion, just like a bright but unchallenged child. Also at this age more than any other, they look to you as a companion in their frolics.

My best advice for keeping your adult Lab happy and in good condition? Wear him or her out every day of his or her life — they'll love you for it. And you'll stay in pretty good shape, too.

IN THE LAB'S OLD AGE, the dog takes on many of the traits of aging humans. They exhibit a gentleness of soul you didn't know they possessed and seem to be grateful for a little attention. And even though they may still have a great zest for life and living, they are also completely aware of the exact time when the afternoon sun strikes the good couch just so, and when dinner is served.

Labs that have spent their lives working, especially as hunters, may be a little stove-up with arthritis (modern medications can help this), a little deaf from time and a lot of close-range gunfire, and slightly blind as their eyesight isn't what it once was. But that incredible nose — the sense that never seems to dim in canines — usually remains sharp right until the end.

At my house, we usually get a pup when the last one to come aboard turns six years old. That way, we have a youngster in training, a dog in his or her prime, and a retired senior citizen snoring away her declining years, usually on the bed with her head on my pillow. The pup will invariably seek out the old dog as an object of puppy-attacks and as a snoozing partner. The pup quickly learns that the dog in his prime usually does not suffer fools gladly, while the older dog is like a grandparent who overlooks faults he once would not tolerate.

The unassailable march of time eventually claims all, including these grand dogs. And when the time comes, as it will, we must be prepared in our minds, if not in our hearts, for what is to come. A pup in the house does not replace the one who has moved on, but it does keep us looking forward to what will be rather than back to what once was.

Breed Characteristics and History

ACCORDING TO THE AMERICAN KENNEL CLUB, THE
Labrador retriever is a member of the "Sporting Group" of
dogs — dogs that owe their origins and heritage to hunting.
The AKC sets strict standards on the appearance of the dogs,
though the general public does not appear to be quite so
picky. The AKC defines a Lab's appearance as follows:

*The Labrador Retriever is a strongly built, medium-sized,
short-coupled dog possessing a sound, athletic, well-balanced conformation that enables it to function as a retrieving gun dog; the
substance and soundness to hunt waterfowl or upland game for
long hours under difficult conditions; the character and quality to
win in the show ring; and the temperament to be a family
companion. . . . The height at the withers for a dog* [male] *is 22½
to 24½ inches; for a bitch* [female] *is 21½ to 23½ inches. Any*

variance greater than ½ inch above or below these heights is a disqualification. Approximate weight of dogs and bitches in working condition: dogs 65 to 80 pounds; bitches 55 to 70 pounds.

The exact specifics of how the dog evolved as a breed are lost in the mists of time. Like virtually all breeds today, Labs are a pinch of this and a dash of that, and a little of something else thrown in because somebody thought it was a good idea at the time. We do know that the dog's roots are found not in Labrador, but in Newfoundland by way of England. In the middle of the 1800s, the fishermen working the waters of Newfoundland had with them a dog they called the St. John's dog, a sturdy animal that probably evolved from something earlier, maybe the old English water dog. From the St. John's dog, the fishermen bred a couple of different strains, one smaller than the other. The smaller ("lesser") went on to become the Labrador retriever, and the larger ("greater") dog went on to become the Newfoundland breed. These dogs were used to help retrieve fish caught in nets (if your Lab brings you a dead fish someday, don't be too hard on him; he's only listening to his ancestral genes). The smaller, or "lesser," breed was also used in waterfowling, which added a little variety to the diet of the locals. Because of these uses, and because of the harsh climatic conditions in this part of the world, they wanted a dog with good retrieving desire, a good coat that would shed water quickly and keep the dog warm in the waters of the cold North Atlantic, and a dog that would be companionable as well.

In Britain, the Labrador retriever is used primarily to mark the fall of game and retrieve it on land, while in North America, the Lab is used as a flushing dog for upland bird hunting — locating and flushing game for the gun — and as the continent's most popular retriever of ducks and geese hunted over water.

The fishermen brought this rootstock dog back to England with them, where a number of the lesser St. John's dogs were used in breeding programs by English gentry looking to develop a reliable gun dog. The fish-and-net-fetching was replaced with a desire to retrieve downed game, because at this time Edwardian shooting parties were at the core of British society's must-do activities. Estates prided themselves on the number of birds brought to bag, while the game was a crop sold at market. Flushing birds for the guns and recovering the downed game was imperative, and the estates on which these shoots were held developed the Labrador retriever as we pretty much know it today. In fact, the legend says that three noblemen, working independently, had each bred a line of dogs that, when merged into one, produced two animals that became the generally recognized progenitors of all Labrador retrievers: Buccleugh's Avon and Buccleugh's Ned. It is also generally felt that this breeding for the gun did not appreciably change the breed from the looks and size of the original lesser St. John's Dog, which, by the way, is also considered the ancestor of all the retrieving breeds.

The Labrador retriever was finally recognized as a breed in 1903 in England by the Kennel Club, but it was not until 1917 when the first Labrador retrievers were registered with the AKC, and about 1927 that the breed was recognized as distinct from the other retrievers in this country (goldens, flat-coats, Chesapeakes), of which only about two dozen were registered. Contrast that with the more than 150,000 registered by the AKC alone in 1999, and you'll be better able to gauge this breed's incredible popularity and acceptance.

The Lab is the most popular of the hunting breeds, while its personality and intelligence make it the ideal family pet.

TODAY, THE LABRADOR RETRIEVER holds on to its hunting heritage as the most popular of the hunting breeds, serving his human partner well in the fields and marshes as a finder and retriever of game. Hunting dogs are great conservation agents, and a dog that can recover downed game — or find it and flush it for the gun in the first place — are highly valued. The Lab's ability to do both makes the breed exceptionally popular among duck and goose hunters, as well as those who specialize in upland game.

But as a pet dog, the Lab has no peer. His personality, intelligence, and loving disposition make him ideal for everyone from the single professional to the suburban family with a raft of kids. Children and Labs, in fact, seem to be inseparable as the dogs are just like kids, willing to try anything if they can just be part of the action.

To get the most from your dog, and to allow the dog to get the most from his life with you, training is important. As we will see as this book unfolds, it is up to you to instill the values of obedience and conformity into your Lab so that his or her life is a productive one. And always and in all ways, this training has to be meted out with love and respect for a dog that has come so far across time to be with you.

Children and Labs seem to be inseparable, as the dogs are just like kids, willing to try anything if they can just be part of the action.

Selecting
a Puppy

THE DILEMMA, SLEEPLESS NIGHTS, AND ULCERS THAT arise when picking your Labrador retriever puppy can be virtually eliminated if you've done your homework in finding the right breeder. There are reasons to worry when it comes to the "backyard" breeder or an acquaintance who suddenly has a litter of pups on his hands, not the least of which are dogs of poor health with mean temperaments. If you want to enjoy your Lab with a minimum of concern, you owe it to the dog to find a reputable breeder, one who cares about the breed, cares about the puppies, and wants to see them go to good homes.

CHOOSING THE BREEDER

YOU MUST FIRST ASK YOURSELF what you want the dog for. Will he be a hunter, a companion dog, a show-ring champion? Or will he simply be a house pet and a family dog? Whatever the answer, you must find a breeder who also has the same goals for his dogs. There is no use choosing a Labrador pup from a breeder who has aggressive, domineering dogs if you want the animal to eventually be a lovable house pet around small children. Also, if you want your Labrador to shine in the field, make sure you look for good hunting bloodlines, with the sire and dam having either field championships or hunting titles in the pedigree. Instincts and temperament have a way of filtering down through the gene pool.

Since you're looking for a puppy, this is a good time to discuss color in Labs. There are three recognized colors: chocolate, black, and yellow. For many years, it was thought that each of these dogs had their own, unique temperaments: the black dogs were thought to be somewhat less intelligent, but more hard-driving and superior hunters. The yellow dogs were reputed to be the smartest but with less drive. The chocolate dogs were regarded as lovable schmoes, good for a few laughs but no great shakes in the field or the ring. Those days, if they ever existed, are long gone. Today, you see dogs of all three colors in the field as hunters and trial competitors, as guide dogs and service dogs, and as intelligent family pets. Pick the color that you figure won't show up on the good furniture, and go for it.

Some yellow Labs get what is known as "winter nose," whereby the color of the dog's nose changes from dark in the summer to lighter, almost pink, in the winter. A few other dog breeds do this as well, and it's not understood why it happens.

Essentially, there are some differences between show-bred and hunting-bred dogs. The show dogs tend to be bred for conformation and temperament, while the hunting dogs — though great companions in their own right — usually have more drive (some would call them hyperactive, although that would not be fair), than their show-ring cousins. Inversely, I have seen a number of show dogs that would and could hunt all day long, do it well, and had to be coaxed back into the truck as the sun went down.

The process of picking a breeder should be done well in advance of picking the puppy. You may have to wait several months for a litter to become available, but this will give you ample time to shop around

It was once thought that the different colors—yellow, chocolate and black—indicated different temperaments. This is no longer believed.

and find the right breeder. Above all, don't choose a puppy on impulse — do your homework!

Labrador retriever clubs and organizations, hunting magazines, or full-fledged kennels devoted to the breed are great places to start looking. Stay away from the breeder advertising a litter of pups in the paper for $40 each. If your friends have Labs that you like, it may be just a simple matter of going to their breeder and putting your name on the waiting list. Once you have found a breeder who takes the business of producing, raising, and placing puppies seriously — above just the urge to make money — then go and meet him or her and see the breeding environment.

It's a definite plus if the breeder belongs to some sort of club or organization that is devoted to the breed. This shows that he cares about the betterment of the breed, and that he is constantly gathering information and talking with other Labrador retriever fanciers about how to produce the best litters. If you want hunting blood coursing through your pup, then it helps if the breeder can display competent hunting skills in the parents, either through pedigrees, hunting titles, or actual demonstrations with the sire or dam. The same applies for show-ring dogs, companion or guide dogs, and family dogs. Speaking of hunting dogs, the breeder, if he is raising gun dogs, will often make noise around the pups — bang some pans and rap on the whelping box — as a way of guarding against later gun-shyness. He is not trying to frighten the pups; he is preventing them from being fearful later on in life.

The breeding environment should be clean. There is no reason to fear the "outside" litter, but one that will be born, whelped, and raised inside will probably have more human contact. And it is imperative to ask how much human contact the pups will get once born. Though Labradors are genetically predisposed to associate with humans, nothing replaces actual human contact in those first few weeks of life. It is vital that they have the exposure. Also, you can get a good indication as to the temperament of the puppies by looking at the dam — she'll be the best litmus test for the pups.

When the pups are born, the breeder should provide documentation of shot and de-worming records, as well as feeding, training, and care instructions; an AKC or UKC registration card; contacts for local clubs, and perhaps magazines or books to help you out. And don't forget a written receipt of sale. You should even be allowed to have 30 days to get the pup examined by a certified veterinarian; if there are problems, get your money back.

Don't be afraid if you get quizzed as to your candidacy to take one of his pups home — in fact, you want this test. It shows that the breeder cares about where his pups are going. He should ask you what kind of dogs you've had before, what your intentions with the dog are (hunting, show, family, etc.), if the dog will be an inside or outside dog, how much time you plan on spending with the pup — in other words, typical nervous parent-type questions. Based on your answers, some breeders will even choose the puppy for you from their observations of the litter through the first seven weeks. Though this is fine, it is nice if you can pick him or her out on your own.

The breeder should provide a four-to-five-generation pedigree for each parent, along with certifications for their hips and eyes.

HEALTH CERTIFICATIONS

THE PARENTS OF THE DOG should have certifications for their hips and eyes, and ideally, their hearts, too. It's a big plus if you can see both of the parents, not just the bitch. The breeder should even have x-ray copies of the parents' hips so you can see that there is no hip dysplasia. Certifications for hips come from the Orthopedic Foundation for Animals (OFA) or PennHIP. As many generations back as possible should also be OFA certified. Their eyes should be certified against retinal dysplasia and PRA (Progressive Retinal Atrophy) by a veterinary ophthalmologist within the previous year (Canine Eye Research Foundation – CERF – certification). The breeder should also provide a four- to five-generation pedigree for each parent.

When it comes to price, now is not the time to be stingy. Accept the fact that, varying by state and location, you're going to pay more to the meticulous breeder who has been breeding for a specific trait (hunting, show, etc.). Though you may find cheaper puppies, you pretty much get what you pay for, and you could end up paying more in medical costs over the dog's shortened lifetime. Better to fork over the

There is nothing wrong with an "outside" breeder, although it is imperative the pups experience human contact, usually by their tenth day.

extra $200 or so on the front end. You may have to put a deposit down, and if you're the first to inquire, this could get you pick of the litter.

CHOOSING THE PUPPY

THE DAY HAS COME. Time to go see the puppies and make your decision. This is usually done when the puppies are around five weeks of age, as this is the time when they are beginning to explore more and are really starting to thrive on human contact. You won't be able to take the pup home until at least the seventh week — or 49th day — but you can pick out the pup now.

The first question you need to ask yourself is, male or female? Answer that based on your intentions. Though you should be extremely careful in deciding if you want to breed your dog and should not enter into that situation lightly, female dogs will carry more responsibility when it comes to having and raising pups. If there are no intentions of breeding, it is recommended that all males be neutered and all females be spayed. Not only will it help control their sexual urges and cycles, it will diminish the occurrences of certain cancers and lead to overall better health for your dog.

Generally, males may tend to be more aggressive; females a bit more laid-back. Males can be a tad tougher and more high-strung when it comes to training (tougher as in they can take it more), while females may require a more gentle hand. Of course, nothing is set in stone; it's better to pick the sex based on your individual preferences. By and large, though, males will err on the hyper side, females on the relaxed.

When you first see the litter together, they should mob you, absolutely thrilled at the sight of people, and *new* people at that. Stand back and observe the litter for a few moments. Is there one in particular that sort of hangs back and doesn't get in the mix? Is there one that is continually shoving his littermates out of the way? You'll want to stay away from both the overly aggressive puppy and the shy, withdrawn pup hiding in the corner. Look for the one that is active, but not bullish.

First, look at the puppies' coats, teeth, eyes, ears, and overall appearance. There should be no evidence of any disease or discharge, nor should there be any bald spots, obvious sores, obvious markings if you care about showing the dog in the ring, or evidence of any adverse reactions to recent shots.

Next, take a few of the prospects individually away from their littermates. Shy away from the puppies that immediately want to return to the whelping box or look distressed in the new surroundings; look for the pups that start to explore their new environment and are precocious to the point of getting into trouble. If you want to hunt your dog, take a duck wing or pheasant tail and tease the puppies with it. Some will immediately be fixated on the feathers and chase it around constantly, even picking it up when you toss it. Other pups will not care one way or the other about what's tickling their nose.

To get a subjective idea of how hard the dog will be to train, roll the dog over onto his back and hold him down with your hand. The pup that struggles constantly might be one tough cookie when it comes to training; conversely, the pup that immediately lies still with a frightened look could be extremely soft, equally hard to train as the blockhead. Try to find the pup that struggles for a few seconds and then lies quietly. This indicates that you can use some pressure in training and not frighten the dog, yet you won't have a battle on your hands. Also, carefully pinch the puppy's toes or his ear to see how quickly he'll react. One that immediately whines could be a soft dog; others will look at you with a, "Is that the best you can do?"

When you pick up the puppy, he shouldn't constantly struggle to get down. He should sit comfortably, content in your presence. Don't expect him to stay that way for too long, but you want to see a little calmness. You also don't want to see the puppy that is constantly biting or growling. Look for the pups that like to hold things or carry them around, and those that respond when you clap your hands or whistle. You should be able to entice a youngster to follow you.

There is no such thing as a "golden Lab," only a "golden-Lab," which is a crossbreed between a Labrador and a golden retriever. The term is most often used to incorrectly denote the yellow Labrador.

Once you've picked out the dog, you'll have to wait a couple more weeks to take the new family member home. Now is the time to buy puppy supplies, make the veterinary appointments, check back with the breeder to make sure the dog gets the last series of puppy shots from him, and prepare your household for the invasion.

Take a crate to the breeder for the puppy's ride home, sign all necessary forms, and get that receipt. Make sure the breeder says it's all right to call for questions about the bloodline, breeding, or the puppy in general, although you don't want to pester him at every turn. If you've been extremely satisfied in your puppy-choosing experience, then be sure to tell the breeder that you'll give him a good recommendation. That's vital to their operation, and reputable breeders help the breed in general. Don't be surprised to hear that the breeder may call in a few months to see how dog life is treating you.

When it comes down to it, picking the breeder is the trick, not picking the puppy. If you've done your homework thoroughly, have obtained many references and recommendations, and have been impressed with the breeding environment and conditions, then you can just about close your eyes, reach your hand into the box, and pick one out. To paraphrase my close friend, the late Gene Hill, you'll end up doing all those puppy selection tests, carefully watching the dogs and selecting the breeder, and then go home with the one that chews on your shoelaces.

REGISTRATION

WHAT'S WITH THOSE SENTENCE-LONG NAMES? Yellow Thunder Josie, Jet of Zenith, Magic Marker of Timber Town, Floodbay's Baron O'Glengarven. Why not just Roscoe? Well, part of that stems from the registration process, a need to give each dog its own individuality, instead of being Abby #92. Most breeders or kennels will attach their kennel name to the dog right on the registration form, with you filling in the name of what you'll call the dog. Others leave it entirely up to you. There's really no science nor a right or wrong way to do it. Just have fun.

Be sure to register your new Labrador puppy with the American Kennel Club or the United Kennel Club. You should have received a registration card from the breeder. Simply fill it out, and send it in along with the registration fee. You'll receive a card with some puppy information in a couple weeks.

Tied in with registration is the new idea of tattooing your puppy or inserting a microchip under the dog's skin. Both are done to identify the dog should he become lost. The chip contains a code that refers to a file in a registry. The microchip, the size of a grain of rice that can be inserted under the skin between the shoulder blades when the puppy is seven weeks old, does not have batteries but shows up under a scanner. The code relates back to the registry, providing information as to the breeder, owner, phone numbers, and even feeding schedules in some cases. Talk with your veterinarian about the advantages and disadvantages of each method, although it is not a requirement that your dog be traced in these ways. However, the chip won't fall off like a collar, and it will provide some level of comfort if your dog should get lost.

The Puppy Comes Home

As you walk in the door with the puppy in your arms, pause briefly at the threshold and take a long, last look about you. Your house and, indeed, your very life will never be the same. Not just because of the toys that you'll trip on, the pup that will always be underfoot, or the gobs of dog hair and muddy paw prints, but also because your home will never again feel as empty, not as long as your new Lab lives and breathes and brings his or her own special character into your life. The squirming puppy in your arms will, from now on, be as much a family member as it is possible for an animal to be, and you will love every minute of it. Well, almost every minute.

This starts the pup's first experience with training and discipline, at least discipline as meted out by someone other than its mother. Here, we should discuss a little canine psychology and social structure. Only recently, geneticists have been able to identify the genes that go together to form this creature we call a dog. What they found was that dogs are actually wolves at the genetic level. Hence, their scientific name was changed from *Canis familiaris* to *Canis lupus familiaris; Canis lupus* is the wolf.

Although there are a number of species of dog — *canids* — in the world, only the wolf has the sort of social structure that people also had developed at the dawn of human history: small family groups of nomadic hunters and opportunists whose rules and behavior patterns were dictated and enforced by the dominant male and female, the Alpha pair. It was no wonder, then, that wolf pups readily fell into the ways of human society — it was like their own, the one their genes told them was the best way to survive.

This is a roundabout way of saying that dogs, and especially pups, not only require discipline, but they want it. You, throughout the dog's life, will be the Alpha animal — unless you abdicate the position and allow the pup to do as he pleases, something neither of you wants. A Lab wants to please, the same way he or she would want to please their mother, and the same way those *Canis* genes would require them to be subservient to the Alpha male or female in the pack. You, quite literally, have become the leader of the pack, and pack leaders maintain their rank and pack order through discipline. Fair and gentle, yet firm, discipline is genetically required by the animal; it is not mean or cruel — only methods are cruel. Making and enforcing rules and being consistent actually comforts the young dog; it makes him feel at home and in his proper place within this new pack. I'll discuss this further later in the chapter.

THE YOUNG AND THE RESTLESS

FOR THE FIRST FOUR OR FIVE WEEKS after you bring him or her home from the breeder, the pup has three things that he must learn: that the inside of your house is not his bathroom (housebreaking), what *no* means, and his name. During that time, you should also mold his desire to retrieve, bond with him, and let him explore and be a puppy. However, the housebreaking and *no* command are vital if you are to enjoy your pup, and if he is to enjoy you. The act of learning his or her name will come in time, provided you are constantly using it and helping him understand that his name means you want his attention. For instance, instead of saying, "Good boy," when he does something right, say, "Good Roscoe," or "Good Maggie."

EARLY HOUSEBREAKING

AFTER SETTING THE NEW FAMILY MEMBER down on the floor, you will be in a constant state of readiness for the slightest indication of the puppy's full bladder. If the little rascal is ever going to be trusted in the house, the pup is going to have to learn to go to the bathroom outside, the all-important lesson of housebreaking. Though it may not seem like it at first, the pup will eventually learn that a full bladder means go to the door. Just be patient.

Some young Labs can have a rather comical way of running called "butt-tucking," where the dog scootches his hindquarters forward and runs with his backside skimming the ground and his head high in the air. This does not indicate a structural problem, but merely seems to be a "Lab happy-run." It's nothing to worry about, and the pup outgrows it eventually.

Housebreaking a puppy is easier if you train yourself to recognize the signs. Watch for the pup that suddenly becomes uninterested in a chew toy, perhaps starts exploring a little too eagerly, or just abruptly looks uncomfortable. Puppies sniffing the floor, especially in a circular motion, are good candidates for going outside quickly, as are those little scoundrels that all of a sudden just disappear as if they are on a secret mission; they are.

There is no use in dragging the pup back to the dirty deed and shoving his nose in it if you haven't caught him in the act. The older dogs become, the more they'll remember; for now, they can't get the hang of their name, much less remember that they wet the floor 10 minutes ago. So if you stumble upon the scene of the crime, accept the blame for not keeping an eye on the pup or taking him outside after he was done roughhousing.

However, if you see the precursors to a puppy having to relieve himself, scoop him up while you say, "Outside!" There may not be time for you to snap a leash on him, but don't worry — at this age, you can usually run him down if he starts to scamper away. Don't let him back in the house until he goes to the bathroom, and when he does go, praise him thoroughly. He has to learn that as soon as he goes, he gets to come back in; the longer he holds it, the longer he has to be out there. Incidentally, this a very good reason why housebreaking in the winter usually takes less time than in the summer. If the pup is freezing his bare belly off, he'll hurry up so he can go back into the warm house; if it's warmer, he'll want to explore more. Also, as you pick the dog up to take him outside, be careful not to lift on his tummy, or you'll be treated to a warm surprise down your leg.

While the pup is doing his business, try adding some commands. Saying, "Hurry up!" as he is urinating, or, "Go potty!" will eventually make the dog relieve himself on command. This is very useful on trips, if you and the dog are staying at a hotel, or when the mercury dips dangerously low and *you're* freezing. You should notice how once he gets his toes in the grass he seems to settle in, maybe wiggling around a bit. Once you see him start to get comfortable, the evacuation will follow. This is a good time to tell him, "Hurry up!" and soon you'll be able to stimulate that sensation simply by the command. It's a nifty trick and can save a lot of time in strange places when the dog is more interested in the smells about him than his bodily functions.

If you catch the pup in the act of going on the floor, then it's time for a scolding. Grasp the pup gently by the scruff of the neck, reprimand with a sharp, "No!" and gently shake her, repeating, "No!" There is no need to swat her behind — a scolding and a gentle shake will get the message across. Quickly take the pup outdoors while you say, "Outside," again, and stay out there with her until she finishes or goes again, praising her when she's done.

ANTICIPATE THE OBVIOUS

IN ADDITION TO RECOGNIZING the signs of when a puppy has to go, you should understand the times when he'll probably have to empty his bladder. The old saying that puppies are nothing more than a hollow tube you pass food through is very true. Almost immediately after mealtime, take the dog outside. What is your first stop when you get up in the morning? It should be the pup's, too, and that goes for after midday naps. If the pup has been quite active for a while — chasing the tennis ball, another dog, or tearing into a rubber chew toy — chances are he's going to have to go when he starts to calm down or gets on his feet. Say, "Outside," or whatever command you want to use to tell him it's time to go out to the bathroom; be consistent, though, and use the same command every single time you take him outdoors.

Don't think that you're going to bring the puppy home and be able to sleep through the entire night. He or she is simply not going to be able to hold it that long. About every two hours, you're going to need to take her outside, even if she hasn't awakened already. Set the alarm for every two or three hours for the first week or so, wake her up, and take her out, repeating the *outside* command. At first, she might want to play when you bring her back indoors, but she'll soon learn that nighttime is the time to restore the energy she'll need to plague you during daylight.

As the pup gets older, start moving the nighttime bathroom breaks back a half hour. Then an hour. Soon, after about two weeks, you might only have to take the little rascal out once or twice. Be sure to always let him go outside if he gets up himself and starts whining — he may have to go again, or his bladder just didn't take three hours to fill up. It's imperative that whenever the dog whines or is trying to get your attention about an impending bladder release, that you get up and take him out. This is precisely what you want him to do — get your attention. You don't want to ignore him or tell him to shut up and go back to sleep.

But how do you recognize the difference between "full bladder" whines and "I-want-to-get-up-in-your-bed-and/or-play" whines? That takes practice, and every dog is different. Some puppies will absolutely insist that they sleep with you; others will be more nocturnal than bats. With repetition and practice, you'll eventually switch the dog to your

schedule. But for now, remember that this puppy is only recently sep-
arated from his mother and littermates, and is in a strange home with
strange people and strange smells. The first thing he'll bond to will be
another dog (if you have one), and then you. Therefore, it makes sense
that when the lights go out and everything gets quiet, he might get
scared and want to be near you. Use your discretion as to how much
of this aid and comfort you want to give, but realize that the more you
give him, the more it will take to break him of it. I'll discuss this further in another section.

Puppies that don't seem to get the hang of being able to hold it
until they go outside may be indicating there's another problem, in
particular a bladder infection. This is when the dog feels like he has to
go all the time — and usually does. Look for the early signs of a dog
that is constantly squatting, even if nothing is coming out. This condition can be easily cleared up with a visit to the vet.

Housebreaking takes time. You need to be patient, and always be
consistent in your discipline, praise, and commands. Always use, "No!"
when scolding and repeat, "Outside!" when the pup goes to the door,
makes the telltale signs, or finishes with one of the aforementioned
events that usually culminates in a full-court evacuation. And when the
dog goes outside, be sure to tell him how wonderful he or she is.

While your new puppy is learning the ins and outs of the house,
her new family, and this housebreaking thing, you'll start to fear that
she's going to think her name is "No." That will be the one word you
will use more than any other in the first few months of dog ownership,
yet it is the one word she must learn — and quickly. *No* will stop her
from biting, chewing, wetting, barking, yapping, yowling, digging,
destroying, leg-humping, and otherwise being a menace to society.

You want to be firm when you say, "No." Stare the dog down and
bark the command. If the little ingrate is biting the hand that feeds
him, gently grab his lower jaw, shake it, and say, "No!" Picking the pup
up off the ground while saying, "No," is also a good way to get the message across that you mean business. A dog likes to have his paws on

If you catch the pup in the act of going on the floor, then it's time for a scolding; however, there is no use reprimanding a dog for something he did five or 10 minutes before—he won't connect the scolding to the deed.

something, to have some sort of foothold. If you take that away from him, he'll freeze and stiffen, and usually, his ears will open up. He'll begin to stop doing the things that will lead to him being off his feet.

HONEST, OFFICER, I WASN'T EVEN IN TOWN THAT WEEKEND

MUCH THE SAME WAY you may have had to "baby-proof" your home, you'll have to "puppy-proof" it also. Closing the door behind you will be the most important thing you can do to keep the puppy out of trouble. Trouble not only means the dog getting into things you don't want destroyed — slippers, papers, your dirty laundry — it also means he's safe from the things that can harm or kill him: poisons, detergents, antifreeze, medicines, sharp or hot objects. And whenever you close the door behind you, not only make sure you didn't shut the puppy inside, but make sure that the door latches. I almost lost a dog (not even a puppy) to a box of rat poison because I thought I had pulled a garage door tight when, in fact, I hadn't checked to be sure. She pushed it open with her nose and ate the poison. That's the day she

Baby gates are a terrific way to block a pup's access to certain areas. Make sure they are close to the floor so a pup can't squirm under them.

was introduced to Mr. Stomach Pump at the vet's office.

Other barricades that are effective are pet gates or baby gates. These come in all shapes and sizes, and they are indispensable for keeping the dog in or out of a room. They are especially useful in a stairway, keeping him upstairs or down in the basement. But realize that some stubborn dogs will not be deterred by a simple gate. Some will lunge over the top; others will chew right through. Use the gate as a form of control, but include times when you can let the dog wander on his own or go into a room (with you) that he's normally not allowed in. If he's always kept out of a certain area and not taught the proper way to behave in those places, then he'll always be a puppy when it comes to that room (or wandering the house). In order for him to behave well with freedom, he has to experience freedom.

MY PLACE OR YOUR PLACE?

OF COURSE, LEAVING A NEW PUPPY free in the house while you leave is nonsense; some dogs will take years of proving themselves before you can trust them to behave without supervision. And the best way to confine the dog when you leave is with a kennel or crate.

Crates literally come in all shapes and sizes; but if you think you'll do any kind of traveling with your dog, be sure to get one that is airline approved. They will have more secure fastenings on the side instead of just simple latches that can be easily removed or unfastened. Unless you want to buy a different-sized crate for each size the puppy grows to, buy the one he'll fit in as an adult — which for a Lab means a large or extra large. You can always use something to partition off half of it when he's a puppy to help with housebreaking (more about this in a bit).

You've perhaps heard the important dog-training rule that you should never use the crate as a form of punishment. You want the pup to enjoy going into his kennel, to see it as his little "bedroom" or his "place." Every time you go somewhere and have to put him in, you don't want him cowering in the corner; if you use the crate in a callous manner, that's exactly how he'll react when you move him toward it.

One way to make the kennel a positive place is to feed him in it. Leave the door open, but place his food in there. Toss treats in the crate for him to run in and get. He'll soon learn to associate the crate with something he craves — food. Leave the crate in an accessible area so that when he starts chewing on a toy, you can direct him there; or if he falls asleep, gently pick him up, and place him in his kennel — with the door open. As you progress, close the door, then eventually latch it. You can use the kennel at nighttime, provided it's not tucked away in a basement far away from the ones he loves. Putting him in his kennel when you travel — something all dogs grow to love — will help him to understand that the kennel can mean good things. And every single time you put him in his crate or if he goes in on his own, say, "Kennel," or whatever command you want to use.

Be sure to let a quiet puppy out of his kennel, and ignore one yapping his head off. He must not be allowed to think he can bully you into doing what he wants.

Sometimes, no matter what we do, the crate is going to seem like punishment. Some days, the little yahoo is more than we can handle, so we stick him or her in the crate so we can get a little peace and quiet. If he's been on a tear — having one of those days — there's hardly any way to put the pup away in his place without having it look like punishment. Just remember to crate him with a cheerfulness that you don't feel. His crate should be a good place.

Make sure you put the crate in someplace warm, especially for little puppies. Don't leave it out on an unheated porch in January in the North; conversely, don't leave it in the only non-air-conditioned room in the house in July. Keep the climate mild for the dog. And while the pup is young, try to keep the crate in an area where he can see you when he's in there.

Your puppy will shred any bedding you put in with him or her, be it a towel, kennel pad, or blanket; that's just a fact of life. That leaves the hard kennel floor. Usually when you buy your kennel crate, there will be thin foam kennel pads available as well. Be mindful, though: puppy pee will soak right through; and unless you want to keep washing it, it might be best to remove it until the puppy has displayed some degree of bladder control. Until then, lining the bottom with newspapers will make some of the inevitable cleanup faster.

It's a good idea to leave a chew toy in there with the dog so he has something to play with. If there's nothing with him, he'll turn those puppy teeth to something else — in a bad case exemplified once again by our wonderful model pup, her own leg. She gnawed on her foot, developing a nasty sore that had to be treated by a veterinarian.

USING THE CRATE FOR HOUSEBREAKING

CRATES REALLY HELP IN HOUSEBREAKING, especially if you partition off half the kennel. When the pup starts to view the crate as home, she won't want to soil it anymore than you'd want her to. If she has room to roam in there, she'll simply go in the corner; if it's blocked off, she'll have to lay in it. Dogs will learn how unpleasant that is very quickly. Canines are normally clean creatures and dislike being near their own waste, so they'll hold it. Listen to the pup's yammering, and determine if she's bored or has to go outside.

You want your pup to view his crate as a positive place— sort of his own little room where he feels comfortable and secure. The crate then becomes a tool for housebreaking, travel and control of your house.

To block off half the kennel, wedge in a piece of wood. You can also use a box or a milk crate, but the puppy may flip these over onto herself or trap herself on the wrong side. Something sturdy and firm that can stand up to puppy pressure — and that you don't mind getting chewed — will work.

HELP ME MAKE IT THROUGH THE NIGHT

AH, IT'S FINALLY BEDTIME for the hooligan, his first night's sleep in his new home. You're bushed. Time to crash and call it a night just so you can get up in the morning and do it all over again. I certainly hope you don't think it will be as easy as drifting off to thoughts of your little misfit all grown up and brining back a pheasant, catching a Frisbee, or launching himself off a dock. It won't be that easy.

Though I addressed some of the housebreaking issues you'll have to deal with at nighttime, there are also the sleeping arrangements that must be reconciled. And be careful — puppies that seem to take weeks to understand their name, months to grasp *sit* and *stay*, and never quite get the hang of *roll over*, will learn, in absolutely Guinness Book record time, that if they whine once, they get to come up on the bed with you. If you don't mind the adult dog sprawling out on the bed next to you, then by all means, let the puppy sleep there. But as soon as the pup sleeps there once, you'll be astonished at how quickly he'll insist on sleeping there permanently. So, you must decide where you want the adult Lab to sleep, and begin there with the Lab pup. If you're going to

want the adult to sleep in his crate in the hallway, then start there. But here's fair warning: Because he's not going to be near you, he'll work those vocal cords to the max, and you'll be amazed at how long the pup will be able to stay awake. It will take much longer for him to sleep through the entire night. Most people prefer to have their dog sleep on the floor in their bedroom. If that's the case, then bring his crate in there with

If you don't want an adult dog sleeping with you, then don't allow the pup to share your bed either, no matter how cute he is.

you. When he can hear and smell you, he'll settle down much quicker; if you already have an adult dog on the bedroom floor, put his blanket or pad next to the puppy's crate. And, as mentioned before, you'll be able to hear when nature calls and he has to go.

For the adult dog, it's a good idea to get a pad or dog bed. Though you probably won't want to trust a puppy to sleep on one until he's housebroken, it's a good idea to let older dogs have one. The bed or pad will provide a haven for them to go to and lie down throughout the day. The pads come in myriad types of covers and stuffing. A pad that can be machine-washed or one with a removable cover that can be washed are the best. Ones stuffed with cedar tend to hold odor a bit longer.

With a Labrador retriever, you may want to stay away from the pads that look almost like dog boxes or beds, the kind with a raised rim around most of it. Labradors like to sprawl out when they sleep, and unless you can find one big enough to accommodate a stretched out 75-pound dog, stick with the traditional pad and let the dog sleep in whatever fashion suits him.

LET THE GAMES BEGIN

YOU CERTAINLY DON'T WANT your new little charge to make a toy out of your antique coffee table. In fact, while he is young, it might be better to put that antique coffee table in a room where he can't get at it. But the best way to give those puppy teeth something to sink into, besides your hand, is to shower him with toys. The more options he has, the more he'll stick with the toys instead of moving on to the furniture or carpeting.

Dog supply catalogs and modern pet stores look like Toys-R-Us stores for canines. There is just about every kind of toy imaginable: those that help the dog's teeth, those that help his breath, rubber, plastic, cloth, fleece, balls, Frisbees, stuffed animals, the list goes on. There is really no science to picking a toy — some your dog will cherish and carry around like a security blanket, others he'll never touch. Most are made of material that, should you have a destructive chewer on your hands and he swallows portions of it, will just pass right through his system. Still, you'll need to monitor his chewing and toss out things that he's seriously tearing into. No matter what you choose, you can hardly go wrong — it all depends on the size of your dog and what sort of chewer he is.

Toys will help keep a bored puppy occupied, especially if he has to be in his crate for any length of time. Some toys have cavities where you can place a dog treat, and the pup will spend the next hour or so absolutely obsessed with getting it out. This is a great way to occupy him when guests are over and you need a dog-free zone for a while.

The supposedly indestructible rubber kongs and their variations are great toys for puppies; those with small protuberances, grooves, and edges will massage itchy gums and clean teeth. And they'll usually last a long time. Choose a size that's right for the pup's age, one that he can carry around into his kennel, onto his pad, or to a favorite sunspot on the carpet.

Be mindful of toys that have noise-makers inside. If a pup's chewing on a fleece-shaped bone and it squeaks, he'll be fixated on finding out what is making that noise. Some dogs will simply chew the toy and make it squeak (and drive you crazy), while others will not rest until they've ripped the toy open and exposed the innards. Make sure you choose your toys wisely; you don't want to have to supply him with a fresh one every few days.

Dogs love to chew on rawhide and may be preoccupied with a rawhide bone for hours, leaving you a little free time.

Chewable rawhides and rope toys look good at first but usually evolve into something stinky and slimy. They start off nice, but soon they dissolve into a blackening, soggy lump of some unidentifiable substance. If you don't mind seeing it around the house, then these toys will captivate a pup's interest, especially the rawhides. Be forewarned, though: If you walk around barefooted and step on one, it's an unforgettable experience.

INTRODUCING THE FETCH GAME

YOU CAN, AND SHOULD, also use the toy to introduce the game of fetch. You can toss anything to her and start to coax her back to you with it, but tennis balls and fleece toys work the best. If you want to have your Labrador be a reliable retriever, then you should never play tug-of-war with her toy. If she thinks that giving the object to you turns into a game, then you'll soon be fighting over a prized duck or pheasant. Whenever the puppy has something that you want, gently pry her mouth open, or tickle the back of her tongue with your finger while you say, "Give," or, "Release," or whatever you choose; I've seen some trainers use "Thank-you," as they take the object from the dog. Praise her lavishly when she gives it up. Soon the pup will learn that if you throw it, she can chase it; and if she brings it back to you, you'll throw it again so she can chase it again. Then you've got a game on your hands and have started a retriever down the right road. In no time, she'll be spitting out the ball in your direction for you to throw again.

A good way to start fetching with your pup is to use tennis balls or a rolled-up sock in a hallway of your home with all the doors closed. That way, when you kneel down and toss the ball or sock, there's only one way to go — back to you. At first, he will try to get past you; pretend you don't notice and praise him for bringing back the object. Soon, he'll love the game and the praise.

LEADER OF THE PACK

ALTHOUGH YOU CHOSE WISELY and didn't pick the most dominant puppy in the litter, you'll still need to establish the pecking order of the household. As alluded to at the beginning of this chapter, dogs are pack animals with chains of command, the leader being the Alpha dog. You are the Alpha, the dog's leader. The quicker you establish this, the easier training will be, and the quicker the dog will bond with you. Now is not the time to try to negotiate with the animal. He must respect your leadership and follow; he'll enjoy a battle of wills as much as you do — which is to say, not much at all.

Signs that point to a dog that thinks he is dominant over you are: growling when you come near; aggressive biting as you try to pet him; ignoring you (once he knows his name and some commands, of course); and an overall stubborn attitude. These *avoidance behaviors* manifest themselves in other ways: yawning, looking away, rolling on the ground and fighting a leash, head-shaking, and more. If you get the feeling that he is trying to manipulate you in some way, don't be fooled and think, "Isn't that cute how he keeps nudging my hand to be petted?" He's telling you, "Hey, I didn't say you could stop petting me!" You need to do things on your terms, not the dog's.

Therefore, you'll need to establish that you're the leader. You don't want the dog to be completely submissive to the point of cowering in the corner. This will happen if you try to establish your dominance with force. You need to use commanding yet calm forms of leadership, ones that don't frighten the dog into thinking he's going to be hurt. He needs to feel he can trust you to ensure his survival.

One of the best ways to establish your Alpha position is at meal-time. First of all, feed the dog after you've eaten. While the puppy is feeding, get down on all fours with him. Pet him, talk to him, and above all, don't let him growl or bite at you when you get near his food. If he does, command, "No!" in a loud voice and take his food away. You should be able to get to the point where he will allow you to open his mouth up and physically take the food out of his jaws. Sticking your head near the bowl and making sounds like you're eating also works; escalate that maneuver into taking the bowl from him and pretending to eat it all yourself. He should sit by and watch patiently for you to finish or give it back to him. If he starts to bite at you or barge his way in, you'll have a fight on your hands. A dog that nips or acts threatening to people when food is around is not to be tolerated. Everybody these days knows a good lawyer, and you have no guarantee the dog won't someday chomp down on a visitor or a child.

However, don't expect too much early on. Remember, he's just been competing with his littermates at mealtime. Expect some competition at first. What you don't want is an aggressive, mean puppy demanding his food back.

If you already have another dog in the house, one that you've established dominance over, then watch what that adult dog does to the puppy. And above all, let the older dog establish its dominance over the youngster. There may be some nasty moments as things get

Will that overly aggressive puppy ever make it in a household? What about that shy wall-flower? Though you took efforts to pick a puppy that fell somewhere between the two, you may not have a choice of the entire litter, and, in effect, be stuck with what's left. If you choose, you could wait for another litter; it all depends on what you want. If you're a hard hunter or field trialer, that intense puppy might not be a bad choice, as long as you expect to have a tougher time training and establishing your role as the Alpha. His aggressiveness and intensity will drive him to many retrieves that other dogs would give up on. In other words, you can always tone down the intensity of a dog, but you can never put it into him. If you're looking for nothing more than a house dog that will follow you around, or as a gift for an elderly person, then the shy wallflower might be a fine choice. Tender training will be necessary to get the dog to learn basic commands and house rules, however. Soft dogs with calm temperaments should also make fine therapy dogs.

sorted out, but don't worry. Unless you have real reason to fear that the older dog will seriously harm the puppy, let them settle it. The older dog will realize how small and fragile the puppy is and won't do anything to severely hurt him. A right smart nip, judiciously administered, usually gets everyone on the same page of the playbook.

Making your pup listen to you, keeping him or her in one place for a period of time, always going through a doorway before her, crating when necessary, and various postures will establish that you are the leader. Getting down on all fours and placing your neck over the pup's and giving a soft growl is a dominance move; if the puppy fights you and tries to get out from under you, be careful. Those teeth and nails are sharp! Once the puppy sits there and accepts you over her, you're on your way to being the Alpha.

If you establish the pecking order early, you'll find very few instances when you'll have a combative dog on your hands. As the pup matures, he'll test you to see what he can get away with, and you may have to reinforce your leadership role. But the dog should immediately remember that you're the boss. And the dog that has been correctly taught the subordinate role will not be a submissive pile of jelly. He'll love having his job! He'll have less to worry about, because there's less he'll feel he has to do to ensure survival. He'll accept training in a manner that says, "What can I learn next?" instead of, "Oh no, not this again!" The more you instill in your dog the feeling that he can trust you to keep him healthy and occupied, the more you'll establish yourself as the leader.

CAN'T WE ALL BE FRIENDS?

NOTHING IS WORSE THAN taking your young dog over to a friend's house and spending the entire time apologizing for his behavior. Sure, new puppies are handfuls; but there will be a point when the behavior is obnoxious. For this reason, you need to properly socialize your dog — with other dogs, people, and environments. Socialization is simply teaching the dog how to behave in human society — how to comfortably and confidently live in your world.

This is done in one simple way: Include your dog in everything! Take him places, let him explore, let him feel his way through his new world. And at first, it's important to let the pup experience these new things on his turf — bring your friends and other dogs to him. As he starts to get bolder, then take him to new places. Insist that your friends not let the puppy get away with things you don't want him to do at home, especially biting. But also be sure they reprimand him the same way that you would. That is another way for the dog to understand that he is not the leader in your absence, and that other people are also dominant over him.

Pups are eager to accept you as the leader of the pack; they are less anxious when someone else is in charge.

Playtime with other dogs is invaluable. You want the pup to be able to romp with other dogs and not have every encounter with another animal turn into a brutal fight. The best way to ensure this doesn't happen is by exposing him or her to plenty of other dogs, especially those their age. Supervise them to be sure they don't get hurt or that two curious pups don't get into something harmful, but just let them play.

Puppy obedience classes are an excellent venue for socializing your dog, as most of these are gatherings of people and their dogs with little strict training. As the pup matures, there are Canine Good Citizen tests, where dogs will be expected to behave in the presence of strangers and other dogs. If your dog is intended for the show-ring or field trial work, getting along with other dogs is imperative. Once, while judging a hunt test, I had to ask a handler to pick up his dog because it was more intent on fighting than with the task at hand; it ruined the handler's day, and it didn't do much for the owner of the innocent, victim dog, either.

Socialization also means learning to get along with other dogs, not just with people.

INTRODUCING THE PUP TO SWIMMING

NOW IS ALSO THE TIME to expose the pup to different surroundings, especially to water. Be sure that the ice didn't just melt when you take him for his first swim. You want the water to be a positive experience. Labrador retrievers seem to have a gene that predisposes them to life in a lake. It won't take much to get a pup to like the water.

When the water is warm enough, at least 60 degrees or warmer, take him down to the shore and just let him romp. He'll soon wade into the water. He'll probably jump back at first, unsure of what that stuff is; but once he learns how fun it is to be in there, you soon won't be able to keep him out. If you have an older dog that loves the water, take that one along — dogs readily learn by example.

Always let the dog go in on his own; never pick him up by the scruff and toss him in. Put on some waders or boots and go out into the water, coaxing him to come in after you. He'll probably just sit

Let a pup wade and get used to water on his own. Playing fetch in the water, with each toss going a little farther, is a good way to gently encourage him to swim.

there and stare at you, so take along one of his toys, preferably one that he absolutely cannot resist. Tease him with it, splash the water, do whatever it takes to get him to come to you, but let him come on his own. At first, the pup will only go as far as he can while still touching the bottom.

Now is when you get him to use those legs to keep him afloat. If the pup is pretty proficient at chasing things you throw for him, toss his toy in the water and let him get it. Keep tossing it farther until he eventually has to swim for it. A slight nudge off his feet into deeper water now is not harmful, provided that the dog already likes the water when he can touch bottom. He'll have a terrified look on his face the first time he's pumping those legs to stay afloat, but with plenty of praise and congratulations, he'll quickly think it's fun. Once he's done that, he'll be busting through the waves for a swim.

The pup will look like a carp out of water at first, probably flogging the water with the front paws and swimming almost vertically. Don't worry; he'll plane out into a champion swimmer. Some dogs won't get the hang of it quickly, though. You can't take a dog to swimming class, but you can give him plenty of exposure to water and let him figure it out on his own.

Do I Look Good or What?

When the pup is little, you also want to get him used to being groomed, in particular around his toes, ears, and mouth; the vet will be looking at those things during regular checkups, and you want a cooperative animal (so does the vet!). Very gently, stick your fingers in his mouth and rub his gums and hold his teeth. Don't do anything to cause pain or anxiety. A puppy comfortable with your hands in his mouth will let you clean his teeth much easier. You'll get those fingers of yours bitten fairly regularly at first, but the pup should get used to being touched on his lips and gums.

Also, gently rub the fur between his toes. Dogs will naturally be ticklish there, but you don't want him to be dancing around when you come at him with toenail clippers. The younger he gets used to having his feet and other groomable areas touched, the easier it will be to keep him looking nice.

If the pup is to be a hunting companion, then you also want to introduce him or her to feathers. These can be in the form of duck wings or pheasant tails, frozen pigeons that you've shot, or birds you've brought back from a hunt. Let the pup experience the tickly feathers in her mouth; toss a frozen pigeon for her and let her tussle over it. As long as you don't let her sit down and completely devour something with feathers on it, you're laying a good foundation for later exposure to birds.

Oh, the Weather Outside Is Frightful

Although it's been established that Labrador retrievers are people dogs and just won't be entirely happy unless they're at your feet, there may be a variety of reasons that you must keep your dog outside. You could be allergic to pet dander; your landlord may frown upon an inside dog but not mind one in a kennel; or you may have too many precious things to trust around an excited, thrashing lead pipe of a tail.

The outside kennel should give your dog at least 10 to 20 feet of room to trot around in, and have a sloped, concrete floor. This will help in cleaning up, but it will also keep soil-borne bugs and mites from infesting the dog. There should also be some form of shade, either from a dog house, kennel cover, or natural shade, and the fencing should be at least five to seven feet high — you'd be amazed at how well these dogs can climb. Also, have a padlock on the kennel door. There are thieves out there, and as was mentioned earlier, Labradors are not the greatest at recognizing dangerous people.

You must have ample water available to the outside dog, as he will probably drink more if he's constantly in the sunshine and heat. Not

When out in the hot sun all day, the pup needs a constant supply of clean water.

having sweat glands, dogs cool by breathing in through the nose and out through the mouth, depending on moisture in both to carry away excess heat through evaporative cooling. You drink when you're thirsty; dogs drink when they're hot and thirsty. If you use a pail, clip the handle to the chain link with a fastener so that your dog can't tip it over. In the winter, you may have to switch to an electronic dog-watering system, one that has an internal heating mechanism so that the water doesn't freeze.

If you make the commitment to have a dog but need/want him to be outside, you must not neglect him in times of weather extremes. Pay attention to the pet warnings on the local news or radio broadcasts. In cases of extreme hot or cold temperatures, they'll recommend bringing any outside pets into the house. You can usually throw his blanket or kennel pad into the basement and keep him down there; if he has some house manners, you should be able to trust him in the house with you. Always be mindful of the weather, and realize that when *Canis lupus* was domesticated, he lost touch with many of the physiological and behavioral traits and characteristics that helped him survive in the wild.

Who's in Charge Here?

I PREVIOUSLY DISCUSSED various commands, in particular *outside, hurry up, no, kennel*, and *give*. Your pup is going to be mobbed with orders and commands throughout his formative weeks; don't expect him to start learning them until you begin to train specifically for those commands. For instance, don't expect the pup to plop the tennis ball in your lap at eight weeks of age the first time you say, "Give."

However, you can begin to lay the foundation for those commands before you begin to specifically train for them. Say, "Give" each time you take something from the dog's mouth, with a prying open of the jaws if necessary; command, "Sit" each time it looks as though the dog is going to sit on his own; say, "Stay" if the pup is just sitting by himself and staying there. Whenever you place the dog in his crate, say, "Kennel," so that when you begin to train for that particular command, the word is familiar to him. Whenever the dog bounds toward you, say, "Come," or, "Here." In all instances, be consistent and use the same word each time, and make sure that other family members also use the same words.

If you let a puppy drag a short cord or leash around while romping through the house, he'll take to leash training much quicker because he'll be used to the collar and leash around his neck.

Above all, you must have patience when it comes to getting the dog to follow your orders. If you're quick to lose your temper, then you shouldn't have brought a dog into your life. Dogs, especially puppies, will test that temper at every turn; they'll make you understand just exactly what patience is all about. Repetition is how you eventually win the battle; getting angry and flying off the handle at a dog that doesn't know what you mean by, "Come" will only set him back and hurt his chances for understanding. There will be times for discipline and a scolding, but above all, patience and repetition will win out.

To help in the eventual training process, make sure you get the desired behavior out of the dog when you're first introducing him to the commands. This is also a good way to further establish your dominance. But if the pup has a ball and you say, "Give," and hold out your hand and then let the puppy just wander off with the ball, you're laying the foundation for a tough training regime. When you say, "Give," even if the puppy has never heard the word before, open his mouth for him and take the toy, praising him when you have it. Every time you say, "Sit," don't let the pup walk away as if he has better things to do than to listen to you. Make him sit. You don't have to be mean about it; just demand compliance. But in that demand, remember that the puppy has no idea what those words mean. You are laying a foundation of commands so that he'll recognize the words, even if just slightly, when you begin to train.

> Say, "Ouch!" whenever the puppy bites you playfully, and act hurt. Soon, the pup will calm down when you say it, thinking that he hurt you. It's a good way to calm a hyper puppy.

Labrador retrievers are *retrievers*, and using toys and playtime when they're puppies to mold that instinct is invaluable. You may find it difficult to get the pup to come back to you once you toss a toy. He may pick it up and go somewhere else, lie down and chew on it, or just ignore it.

When you first toss it, let him chase it madly, but say the command you'll later use to release him for a retrieve. This could be "Fetch," or his name. To get him to come back to you, keep whistling, clapping, and calling his name, saying, "Come!" while you move into a different room, out of sight. Most often, the pup will come tearing around the corner to see where you've gone; and most often, he won't have the object with him. That's okay — once you get a few puppy retrieves out of him and praise him lavishly, he'll start to learn that he needs to keep the object with him when he comes to see you. But moving out of sight will help get the pup back on his feet and running to you. Also, if he is attached to his kennel or has an otherwise "favorite spot" that he always runs to with his toy, get between him and that spot. That way, he'll scamper right at you on the return trip; you can scoop him up, praise him, and keep the game going.

Even if you don't have plans on hunting the pup and aren't worried about gun-shyness, you should get him used to loud noises. This will help especially when a thunderstorm rages outside or the neighbor kids are shooting off firecrackers. To accustom the pup to loud noises, make the noises go hand-in-hand with something he likes, i.e., his food or his toys. While he's gobbling up dinner or chewing his fuzzy guy, clap your hands once or twice and then praise him; escalate to banging a pan or slamming a cupboard door. Do it only once or twice; he doesn't need to feed to a cacophony of pans, doors and applause. If you do plan on hunting him, eventually escalate the noise level to firing a blank pistol far away from the dog, and gradually move closer to him. Also incorporate loud noises when you play fetch with him. Whatever you do, never frighten a pup with loud noises — don't wake him up with a stomp on the floor, sneak up on him from behind and pop a balloon, or pound on his crate with him inside.

Three Squares

It goes without saying that you must always have clean, cool water available. But the question of what to feed a dog is one of the most controversial topics in the dog world, mainly because there is a lot of money to be made by the various companies; the pet-food business is a several-billion dollar annual enterprise.

First, understand that Labradors fall into the category of large breed. Dog food companies are now starting to categorize their blends into large breed, small breed, senior dog, and so on. For the most part, any of the commercial brands on the market have proven themselves time and again. It is hard to go wrong in following the different blends and feeding schedules for your dog's age and weight.

> *Avoid feeding your dog chocolate at all costs, especially if it's unsweetened! Chocolate contains* theobromine, *a substance that is toxic to canines.*

Some of the premium, more expensive foods may have blends that are more specialized; for instance, a puppy large breed formula. Some are designed for active dogs, which require a bit more protein when they're working.

When it comes to dry versus canned dog food, dry food produces firmer stools and cleaner teeth. For small puppies, it is important that you soften dry food with warm water, because their tiny teeth and jaws are not strong enough to crunch the kibble yet. Mixing canned with dry food is also a good way to soften the food and make it easier to go down the hatch.

One big food controversy is the question of whether a puppy formula will cause the dog to grow too fast, thereby causing bone and joint problems. There is some scientific basis for these claims, especially for the large breed dogs. And a diet especially high in protein can be a factor in these developmental problems, as well as too much calcium and other nutrients. But many foods have formulas that are balanced for all puppy breeds, with adjusted feeding rates depending on how big the dog will reach at maturity.

Insofar as nutrients and food ingredients are concerned, you first want to look at the protein. For a Labrador retriever, an active large breed dog, the range for an adult should be somewhere between 21 to 26 percent, depending on the season (more during active times; less in the off-season). You can switch to a higher-protein diet come hunting season when the dog is older, but don't overload a puppy with protein. A pup that seems to be growing unbelievably fast could be developing structural problems as a result.

Remember: Dogs are omnivores, leaning toward carnivores. Therefore, don't insist that he become a vegetarian; look at the animal matter contents of the food as these provide most of the amino acids necessary, remembering that the first ingredient listed is the largest by volume in the blend. There should be at least a few different animal products (lamb, chicken, beef) in the food, balanced with byproducts and cereal grains, which deliver the amino acids the animal products don't. Try to stay away from foods that have many variations of the same type of grain (especially rice products).

Next, look at the fat content. Unlike humans, dogs thrive on fat. It helps their coats, is a great source of energy, and makes a better-tasting food. You must be careful, however, as fat in extreme amounts will lead to obesity. For Labradors, a food with eight to 10 percent crude fat content will deliver the necessary requirements for an adult.

Too much protein in a pup's diet can cause her to grow too fast, leading to developmental problems in the joints and bones.

Remember to guard against this with the pup, as you don't want him growing at an alarming rate. If using a food with less fat than this, you can try mixing a teaspoon of vegetable oil with it every so often. This is especially good to do during his working season.

Be aware that changing foods many times until you find something you and the dog like won't be the best for your puppy's stomach and could lead to diarrhea or make him a finicky eater. Try to find a good brand and formula and stick with it. If you do find yourself switching brands, incorporate the new formula slowly, mixing it with his normal food first, eventually switching completely over to the new diet. You can move to an adult food when the puppy is around six months old. In the end, it is hard to go wrong by choosing a respected brand and following the schedules published on the bag.

There are many different feeding dishes on the market — plastic, stainless steel, ceramic. Some are even raised off the floor to promote better digestion. Whatever you choose, you may want to shy away from the plastic food dishes. With ravenous eaters such as Labrador retrievers, they may eventually get small plastic splinters in their chins. A ceramic bowl is easy to clean and heavier, so the excited pup won't push it all over the floor. Stainless steel bowls stack easily for travel.

Once you've decided on a brand of puppy food, it's time to set the dish down. First of all, you're making the right decision by setting the dish down. For Labrador retrievers and other large breed dogs, it is unwise to allow the dog to be a self-feeder. If you constantly keep the pup's bowl full, the pup will constantly be full. Labs are voracious eaters, and most will keep eating as long as there is food available or until they burst into black, yellow, or chocolate bits. Though you've probably heard exceptions to this, there are very few things that can go wrong if you set up a feeding schedule. If you allow self-feeding with a dish that constantly has food in it, the number of problems that can occur rises drastically. Better to be safe and set a schedule.

Puppies will need to be fed often while they're young, but usually no more than three times a day; try your hardest to stick to the same times each day, which helps with housebreaking. For instance, just after your mealtimes are the perfect way to remember. This means that you may have to come home from work at lunchtime for a while, but you should anyway to let the dog out of his crate to go to the bathroom — Lab people call it "airing" the dog. Usually, feeding times of around 7:00 a.m., noon, and 7:00 p.m. work best.

When he reaches about four or five months, start to make the midday meal smaller and smaller, putting more food into his first and third meals, until you can phase out that second meal completely. Then, you'll be on a good, two-meal-per-day schedule. And don't forget to follow the label on the food bag closely — you don't want to be feeding him three cups of food per meal when it says per day. Is once a day feeding okay? Yes, and millions of dogs are happy as clams with that schedule. If you do feed once a day, make it the evening meal; a full dog relaxes and rests better.

Aside from helping to control weight, setting a feeding schedule assures that the pup will be hungry when you put the food down. You'll be grateful for this when you're on a trip and you must feed at a certain time. If he's used to having to gobble his food in five or 10 minutes, he'll be prepared for when you set the dish down instead of lingering over it. Setting a schedule helps in housebreaking, because you won't have the food constantly moving through the puppy; you'll know when it's in there and about when it has to come out. The pup will begin to learn that right after mealtime means going outdoors.

When you've done it properly, you should just about be able to set your watch to his stomach. He'll start to come get you when his tummy grumbles; for this reason, don't get him started eating too early in the morning. You want to be able to sleep in at least a little on the weekends!

Guard against the obese puppy. You want to be able to see the pup's ribs, and when you look down at him from above, he should have a distinct hourglass shape. A profile view should show his deep chest rising up to a thinner belly. The more effort you take to control his weight right from the beginning, the better off you'll be when he grows into his bones. He'll look gangly at first — all puppies do. But if he just looks abnormally shaped (extremely gaunt, a round ball, etc.),

pay attention to his diet. A reputable puppy meal will deliver the balanced diet necessary for the dog, no matter the breed.

Keep the puppy on dog food; don't get him into the habitat of begging from the table. Also, and very importantly, don't allow the pup to romp or swim right after eating. This can lead to something called *gastric bloat*, where gas is trapped in the pup's stomach, which then twists, trapping the air. It is a truly life-

Ceramic or stainless steel food and water bowls are preferable to plastic.

threatening — usually fatal — situation. Therefore, you may need to crate an especially hyper puppy to keep him calm after mealtime. Also avoid excessive exercise before his meals for the same reason.

Training and Obedience

THE FOUNDATION OF ALL TRAINING IS ROOTED IN FOUR commands: *sit, stay, come,* and *heel*. Some trainers like to combine *sit* and *stay*, or even *come* and *heel* into one word for both commands. I'm going to use them singularly because I feel it communicates what you want from the dog more clearly. If you use *sit* to mean *sit* and *stay*, then how do you reprimand the pup when he sits but doesn't stay? He followed part of the command — how is he to know which part he is doing wrong? Those who use one command to mean both often do a good job of it; they are probably better trainers (or have smarter dogs!).

Training should be administered with equal parts insistence and praise: Insist the dog do it right, and then praise him when he does. Labs love praise.

As with all training, these four simple commands need to be practiced over and over. The famous Labrador retriever, King Buck, two-time National Field Trial Champion, was

In order for your Labrador to be labeled a Canine Good Citizen by the American Kennel Club, he must be able to: sit quietly next to his owner who's talking with a friendly stranger; allow a friendly stranger to pet him; allow a stranger to examine and/or groom him; walk nicely with the owner with two stops, a left turn, right turn, and about turn; walk through a crowd; do a simple sit, stay *and* down *on command; come when called; have a polite, controlled reaction to meeting another friendly dog; be confident and cool amid distractions; and finally, behave himself while being left alone with a friendly stranger for a short period of time. Does your dog have what it takes?*

trained on *sit, stay, come*, and *heel* every day, even after he had filled the trophy case at the famed Nilo Farms where he made his home. Remember, repetition is the key, and training usually need be no more than five or 10 minutes a day, maybe a morning and an evening session, starting when the pup is 10 to 12 weeks of age. The dog will learn much more quickly in short bursts than in long, drawn-out battles of will. Keep the sessions fun, positive, and rewarding, and the pup should be well on his way to laying a firm foundation for future, and more specialized, training.

It is important to remember to be consistent while training. If you want the pup to remain seated on *stay*, then stick with that command. Don't use *stay* one day and *freeze* the next. If *come* is used to call the dog, don't expect him to race toward you when you holler, "Here!" It's very confusing for the dog when you throw in unnecessary words, expecting the dog to pick out the one you want him to follow. Second, be firm and blunt. "Sit" means *sit*, not "come-on-boy-sit-down-come-on-you-can-do-it-sit-boy-come-on." It's, "Sit."

Also, though many people may handle the dog and give him commands over the course of his lifetime, it's best to train the dog one-on-one. That's not to say that a few people can't train the pup (as long as they also use the same commands you started with and train in the same manner), but during a training session, you don't want your spouse, children, and the odd nosy neighbor hollering commands at him. Take the dog off by yourself and work with him. If your spouse wants to train, don't poke your nose in. A popular saying is that dogs are just children with fur; their attention spans are about the same. The pup will pick up more quickly on commands if he only has to pay attention to one voice giving the instructions.

REWARDS

THERE HAS BEEN MUCH DEBATE over the question of whether you should use food "treats" while training. While food rewards do help to get the message across faster (the quickest way to a dog's brain is through his stomach), they can become a nuisance, especially after you run out of dog bones. Rewarding the pup every fifth or sixth time with a small treat usually works the best as it keeps him guessing — "Maybe this will be the time I get the biscuit!"

A treat can help in training, but some experts advise against it.

Using food is also a good way to teach the dog to depend on his nose to help him find things. My daughter taught her retriever to find a *dead bird*, a useful hunting command, by hiding pieces of hot dog in the grass in her backyard. She first made it easy for the dog to find the food when she was teaching the command, then once the dog knew that *dead bird* meant that she had to get her nose down and find the hot dog, the hiding places became more difficult. As the dog matured, *dead bird* didn't mean hot dog anymore — it meant a duck, pheasant, grouse, or retrieving dummy that was concealed.

Don't get into the habit of repeating a command until the dog obeys. Sure, it's all right to maybe say it a second or a third time, especially if your young pup is not paying attention to you. But be firm — if the pup doesn't sit after one or two commands, show him how it's done while giving the command again. If he's wandering off as you holler, "Stay," don't turn it into a shouting match. Corral the dog, sit him down, and say, "Stay," even if you only gave him the one chance to obey. Repeating the commands is necessary when teaching them for the first time, but after you're sure the pup knows what you mean when you say, "Heel," she should follow the first time you say it.

The command and control system is much easier with a leash or checkcord — a six-foot-length piece of quarter-inch rope attached to a collar is plenty. A so-called "choke chain" collar is handy as well. This collar is misnamed; it should be called a "pop collar" instead, because the way it's used, you simply pop the dog with a quick flick of the wrist or a slight upward pull. The chain will tighten and then loosen quickly, administering a little discomfort and showing the dog that you are calling the shots. For example, the dog has on the collar attached to the checkcord: "Come,"(dog ignores you) — "Come," *pop*, "Come." He'll come.

It helps to get on the dog's level when you begin training. You won't be such an imposing figure if you're on your knees looking the pup in the eyes instead of towering above him. You've already established who the leader of the pack is, so he'll respect you no matter where you are. But by being at eye level, you take yourself out of a threatening position and put yourself into his zone.

DISCIPLINE

ONCE THE DOG KNOWS the commands and has proven he can follow them, discipline will get the message across that disobedience will not be tolerated. But discipline does not mean a beating. A quick ear pinch or a firm scolding are usually all it takes. In the litter, when Mom wanted to discipline the pups, she did so with a nip on the ear. Dogs accept this form of pack discipline without holding a grudge. The *canids* do not, however, smack each other around or paddle each other's backsides, so this form of discipline is usually much less effective than the kind they are genetically engineered to understand. Instead of disciplining the dog while you're teaching a command, give him a firm, "No" when he begins to disobey, and start over (see Stay, below).

The following four commands form the basis for obedience, and they are the ones by which you will train a Lab if he is to follow his heritage and be a hunter. They, of course, are useful as pure obedience commands as well. Other, purely obedience commands, are covered later in this chapter.

SIT

SIT IS A GOOD COMMAND TO START WITH — it's easy, the dog usually masters it quickly, and as you'll see with just about anything you want to teach the dog, you can use his appetite to your advantage. However, it's best to start off without the food and show the pup what you mean when you tell him, "Sit."

With a leash on the pup's collar (if the pup is fairly big) or by grabbing the slip link in the pop collar, pull up at the same time you push down on his bottom. As you do this, command, "Sit" in a firm, but not threatening, voice. When the dog has his rear end planted, praise him, scratch his ears, or rub his neck. Using the leash or collar again, get the pup back on all fours, maybe walk him around a bit, and then repeat the pull up-push down maneuver, repeating, "Sit" each time you do so.

To teach sit, *hold a piece of food or a tennis ball in front of the dog's nose and push down on his bottom. Command, "Sit" as you do this.*

As the pup progresses with this command, incorporate a short delay between when you issue the command and when you pull up-push down — give him a chance to do it himself. Don't expect the pup to do it properly after only a few repetitions; only after perhaps the third or fourth training session and a few-dozen repetitions should you give him the opportunity to respond on his own. Don't get angry if the puppy doesn't do it, or do it quickly enough for you. Remember to have patience. This is a brand new world to him, with new people, smells, surroundings, and lessons.

Once it's obvious that the pup is starting to get the hang of things, mealtime is the perfect opportunity to see success and give a nice reward. Stand up with the full food dish, the dog facing you, and command, "Sit." If the dog doesn't obey right away, hold the dish out and move it back over his head, forcing him to lean well back. When it looks like momentum and gravity will push his bottom down, repeat, "Sit." He should easily sit. Make him stay in that position for a second or two, and then praise him and give him his food. When the pup learns that the sooner he obeys, the sooner he gets something nice, you've got him. As he matures, the "something nice" will be another throw of the tennis ball, a warm feathery duck or pheasant, or the kind tone in your praise.

STAY

STAY IS THE NEXT NATURAL COMMAND to teach, as it builds on and helps to reinforce *sit*. *Stay* and *come* can usually be taught at the same time; but when starting out, stick with one command and use some other cue to let the dog know that he can move again. As stated elsewhere, some trainers do not teach *stay*, making the valid point that *sit* means "sit until you are told to do otherwise." But for those who wish to use *stay* as an additional command, here's how it's done.

Once the dog sits, command, "Stay" and hold your hand out in a stop position like a traffic cop.

The pup should be sitting reliably before you move on to *stay*. *Stay* is best taught, at first, with the checkcord on. Once he is in place, command, "Stay," holding your hand up in front of him in the "stop" position like a traffic cop. This is an important command, and you must be firm. *Stay* may one day keep the dog from bolting in front of traffic, stop him from mobbing guests, or keep him out of broken glass or another kind of danger.

After commanding, "Stay," move a few paces away — so he can still see you — repeating, "Stay" after a few-seconds' pause. Most of the time, he'll look at you with a cocked head as if asking, "Just exactly what are you saying?" As soon as you see the pup begin to move, you might clap your hands, whistle, or do something to tell him that it's all right to move, and also get down on his level. He'll usually bound toward you if he's been paying attention. If he's not looking at you as you're teaching, you're wasting your time. You need to get his attention first before anything good can happen.

Slowly back up after commanding, "Stay," repeating the command after a slight pause.

Increase the time you require the pup to stay in one place as you progress, and increase the distance you move away before you let him off the hook. When he starts to hold in the *stay* position longer, correct him when he moves. As he gets up say, "No," take him by the leash back to the position where he started, tell him, "Sit," and repeat, "Stay." Each time he moves without permission, say, "No," take him back to the starting point, and begin again. You'll soon get an indication as to how long he'll hold in one place on his own before he gets fidgety. Time your release command for just before he starts to move.

After you command, "Stay," be silent. It's not very constructive to set the dog up to fail by throwing in distracting conversation before he has the commands down pat. When the pup matures in his training, you should be able to tell him, "Stay" and carry on with your business; but for right now, it's best to make the sessions as easy for him to succeed as possible. Not only will he learn faster, but he'll bond with you quicker because he'll begin to see just exactly what he has to do to make you happy.

Once the dog can sit *and* stay *reliably, then add the* come *command to break the stay command. Eventually, he'll come when he's called no matter what he's doing.*

COME

YOU CAN BEGIN INTRODUCING THE COMMAND *come* or *here* whenever you're playing with the pup, taking him out for a bathroom break, at mealtime — whenever. But don't expect results until you start working specifically on the command.

To get the pup to come reliably, he'll need to be focused on you. Therefore, trying to teach the dog *come* while he's chasing butterflies, wrestling with another puppy, or terrorizing the neighbor cat will be futile. The best way to have the pup focused on you is by having him *sit* and *stay* consistently, with a leash and collar.

Teaching the dog *come* is nothing more than adding the command to move after the *stay* command. Instead of getting him to bound toward you from the *stay* position by whistling or clapping your hands, simply substitute the command *come*. As soon as you see him start to break the *stay* command, tell him, "Come," and praise him. It's all right at this point to add in some clapping while you give the command, but try to just use the word as soon as possible. Repeat the *sit* and *stay* routine, move away, and again command, "Come." Soon, you'll be able to correct the pup for breaking the *stay* command without it confusing him — he won't think he's being punished for coming as long as you don't say the command while you're reprimanding him. Remember, simply say, "No," lead him back to where he was supposed to stay, walk back to where you were, pause, and command, "Come."

At first, don't be surprised to see that the pup will only come to you from that *stay* position. Don't worry — he'll mature and soon come when he's called no matter what he's doing. Use the leash to help guide the dog to you; don't drag him kicking and screaming. More than likely, if he is good at staying, you'll need the leash to get him started when you say, "Come." Up to this point, you've been making a general commotion when you want him to come; now you're just using one firm word. The pup will need a little encouragement to get started, and a soft pull on the leash to pull him up on all fours will do the trick. Keep repeating and increasing the distance you move away from him.

If you practice this indoors, try moving into another room where the pup can't see you — most times, he'll get anxious to see where you've gone and come looking for you. As soon as you suspect he's moving, say, "Come," and clap your hands so he can find you. He'll have a most relieved look on his face when he comes around the corner and finds you there.

Heel *should be taught when the pup is a little older, and has a good foundation of* come *and* sit.

Heel

Heel is a vital command if you want to enjoy taking the pup for a walk without it being a tug-of-war. The *heel* position is also where the retriever starts when making formal retrieves on marks and blinds. But he'll need to be a little older before you begin teaching *heel*. The pup will need a good foundation of *come* and *sit* before you can expect him to be a good citizen at your side.

With the leash on, start walking with the pup,

Keep walking and saying, "Heel," whenever the pup is by your side. If he lags behind or bounds ahead, say, "No," turn away from him and command, "Heel" again, guiding him back into position.

commanding, "Heel." If he trots up next to you and starts walking by your side, congratulations; but you haven't won yet. He is just following the leash or following you, and not responding to the command at all. Once again, this skill requires repetition.

As you walk, and as he keeps walking by your side, repeat the command, "Heel." Pause and give a rub on his side with, "Good Roscoe" while he's in the correct position. If he starts to bound ahead, hold the leash firmly and let him run to the end of it — don't jerk him back! The pup has a fairly fragile neck, and you don't want to snap him around by it. Just hold tight and let him jerk himself off his feet. When the pup gets to the end of the leash, say, "No," turn away from him, and command, "Heel" again, guiding him back into position. If the pup lags behind, say, "No," lead him into position, and command, "Heel" when he gets into the right spot. Just keep walking and saying, "Heel" whenever he's by your side.

The pup getting ahead of you or behind you is easier to correct with the leash than when the dog wants to bolt off to the left or right. In those cases, find a handy wall such as a house or fence, and *heel* the dog between you and the wall. The wall cuts down on his options. Properly, the dog's head should be even with your knee — no farther ahead or behind than that. For the dog that gets ahead, pop him back with the leash. For the dog that lags behind, hold the leash in your off hand (the side opposite from the dog), and let it pass across the front of your legs to the dog's collar. Now, every time you take a step, your leg will push the leash forward, pulling the dog forward. They catch on to this pretty quickly.

Whether you want the pup to heel to your right or left side is entirely up to you, but be consistent. Most hunters like to have the dog heel on the side opposite where they carry their gun so the dog won't bonk his head on the barrels. I'm right-handed, so I have my dog heel on my left — I carry the gun in my right hand, plus I throw training bumpers with my right hand. I don't want to swing the dummy around and rap my dog upside the skull.

Keep repeating the *heel* command until the pup will walk nicely next to you. Scold if he lags behind or lunges forward, but don't forcefully yank him back with the leash. Soon, use the *heel* command to put the dog into position when he comes to you. Put all four commands together in this sequence: Command, "Sit;" command, "Stay" as you move away; wait a few seconds; say, "Come" to get him to move to you; and as he gets near, command, "Heel" to get him to your side. When he does, finish it off with another, "Sit," and you've got it — a dog that will *stay* when told, *come* when called, and *sit* at *heel*. Whew!

Progressing with the Four Commands

When the pup has displayed at least some level of cognizance of all four commands, work from the *heel* position. While he's walking on heel, stop while commanding, "Sit." You may have to pull up on the leash and push on his butt to remind him what it means. With many repetitions of this, you'll be able to stop walking and have him sit without your saying a word. After he sits, command, "Stay," walk away, and say, "Come" to get him to you. If you want him to move into the *heel* position, tell him, "Heel," and guide him with the leash; once there, say, "Sit" again to finish it off. Start your walk again, and keep repeating these commands in any sequence you like. Again, doing this training near a fence or the house, with the pup in the middle, will help keep him straight.

When the pup really has the commands mastered, you should be able to tell him, "Sit," and keep walking. At first, the dog will want to keep up next to you; just turn around and tell him, "Sit," again and, "Stay," and keep walking after he's in position. This will take a little while to perfect, because the dog has been taught to keep up with you during *heel* training. Now, you're asking him to stay put while you keep walking. It's confusing, and he's likely to look and act bewildered. Don't despair; keep at it, and he will pick it up — just not in the first five minutes.

Whistle Training

Most hunters and trainers use a whistle to give instructions to the dog when he's at a distance that makes shouting difficult or impossible. Whistles also carry much better through the wind, and the dog can pick up the high trill more easily than your voice. Whistle training is not difficult, and you can start it at a young age, but only after the dog understands the spoken command.

The *whistle-sit* is one such whistle command (there are others) used as a substitute for the spoken command. It is introduced the same way as the other whistle commands. The *whistle-sit* command is normally one sharp blast on the whistle, while a *come* whistle command is several short, quick blasts.

When the pup can sit with confidence, introduce the whistle. Command, "Sit" and as he starts to sit, give one sharp blast on the whistle. It'll ring your ears at first, but a sharp blast is the same as a firm spoken command; a wimpy whistle is like asking the dog if he wants to sit instead of telling him. Use the whistle just after you say, "Sit." Even though the pup will sit reliably, it's nice to remind him

Labs, like all canines, have a language they use to express their displeasure with training. Such reactions are known as avoidance behaviors, and present themselves in a variety of ways. Essentially, the dog is either trying to avoid the response the trainer is trying to elicit, or — in more extreme cases — attempting to exert dominance over the trainer. In avoiding the trainer's wishes, some dogs, among other behaviors, will: yawn; look away and refuse to make eye contact; ignore the command as if he has not heard it; shake his head; sneeze; roll over on his side; fight the leash; or yowl as if you're killing him at the slightest physical correction. The dog attempting to exert dominance may try to step on or stand on your feet, show his teeth, growl, attempt to bite, or become seethingly sullen.

with the pull up-push down maneuver when you give the whistle. After many repetitions, start to phase out the verbal, "Sit," and just give the whistle blast. You'll be surprised how quickly he'll understand that there are now two commands that mean the same thing.

SOME FINAL BASIC TRAINING WORDS

THROUGHOUT YOUR TRAINING SESSIONS, there are going to be times when the pup doesn't feel like doing anything productive. Ever have a bad day at work? This is the same thing. The dog's job is to learn and to listen to you. There may be a variety of reasons he doesn't feel like working — he could be sick; having some growing pains; maybe he's tired. More than likely (like the kid he is), he just wants to play.

As a trainer, you need to read your dog. You need to recognize when the pup seems to be a sponge and will soak up anything you tell him; but also notice when your commands are just bouncing off his skull. When the dog is young, you must capitalize on those sponge times, and play and bond during the other times. When the pup matures, you should be able to make him listen when you want him to.

Before mealtime — an hour to an hour and a half before, not a few minutes — is a good time to train. The pup usually isn't hearing his grumbling stomach, and he's probably already had his afternoon nap. It's easy to mold a playing session into a training session if you've been keeping everything fun for him. You also need to recognize when he's had enough. The five- to 10-minute rule is about the maximum for young puppies. Older dogs can go longer; but regardless of age, keep training sessions short in hot weather, even when it's simple obedience training. Whatever the length, be sure you end on a positive note. However, don't endure a couple of bad experiences to get that positive note. For instance, let's say the pup is heeling, coming, and staying like a pro, and you want to get one more good series out of him. But the next couple times, he didn't come right away or sit when you told him to, and you had to reprimand him. Because you really want to end on a positive note, you keep drilling it into him, forcing him to obey the commands when it's obvious that he's finished for the day. If you get into this situation, pause for a few seconds, let the pup romp, and then give him a simple *sit*, helping him with the pull up-push down maneuver. When he does it, praise him, and let him chase you back to the house for dinner.

What you should've done, though, is recognize the signs that the pup was getting ready to quit. Sometimes, he may not come to you as quickly, or he'll sit a little slower after the command. Perhaps he didn't hold his *stay* as long, or you don't get the eye contact you were getting earlier. If you start to see these signs, wrap it up. It's best to keep the dog wanting more and enjoying himself instead of going through a few sharp disciplines before calling it a night. You want him bounding at your side when you grab your whistle and his leash, not curling up in a ball and yawning.

ADDITIONAL COMMANDS AND TRICKS

LABRADOR RETRIEVERS ARE intelligent animals that, at maturity, are able to understand a fairly extensive vocabulary and variety of commands. You can teach a Labrador to do just about anything you set your mind to. Some dogs can be taught to fetch the paper right out of the mailbox (not on busy roads, of course), others can be instructed to open the refrigerator and retrieve a soda for a thirty master. The sky's the limit when it comes to tricks; all you need is patience and plenty of repetitions.

OFF AND DOWN

Both *off* and *down* are important commands that the pup should learn. I have included them in this section rather than the one dealing with *sit, stay, come,* and *heel* because those other commands form the basis for teaching the hunting commands. The *off* command is for obedience only, and is especially useful for keeping your black, yellow, or chocolate pal off your guests (nothing like two muddy paw prints on the shoulders of a white shirt or blouse to enliven a visit from the in-laws).

When you give the down command, move your hand to the floor, and lower your body to show him what you want.

In its simplest form, the *off* command teaches the dog not to jump on people. You must react quickly to the negative behavior in order to correct it, and you'll have to be forceful with the dog. Jumping up on people is a destructive behavior that must not be allowed; it can be dangerous, especially around small children and the elderly.

When the pup jumps up, lift a gentle knee in his chest and say, "No! Off!" while pushing him backward. With an especially enthusiastic jumper, you may even have to grab his paws and throw them backward, almost making the dog flip right over on his back. Another method involves sliding your foot forward around the offending beast and firmly stepping on the toes of a back foot — just don't apply too much pressure. The sooner your dog gets the message that getting up on two feet is unacceptable, the sooner he'll want to stay on all fours. You can also lay a firm foundation for not jumping on guests by demanding that the pup sit whenever he hears the doorbell or new people come into the house. Let visitors go see the dog, not the other way around.

Getting the pup to lie down is nothing more than helping him into the position while giving the command, the same way you taught *sit*. While the pup is sitting, tell him, "Down," take his front paws, and move them forward, bringing the dog to the floor. It helps to be on his level when you teach this; when he's older, keeping the dog on an extended *down* is another great way to assert your Alpha position. When you've helped him into the *down* position a few times, stand a few paces back; when you command, "Down," move your hand to the floor and lower your body. This shows the pup what you want him to do without laying a hand on him. Soon, he should lie down whenever you say the word, regardless if he has a visual cue. Once he is in the *down* position, you can command, "Stay," and he should stay put. You'll need many repetitions of this to get it right.

Leave-It

Another useful command — *leave-it* — is exceptionally easy to teach. *Leave-it* teaches the pup to drop what he has in his mouth. Hunters will often use *leave-it* when they have shot a bird and the dog insists on mouthing it in the blind or boat.

Simply put, when teaching this command, you must show the dog what you want — or don't want — him to do. If you want the dog to *leave-it*, take the offending object away from him while giving the command. Eventually, you won't have to help with the process; the command alone will do it. It's really pretty simple.

Frisbee

This may not be the best trick to teach your dog if he's a hunter. You've been instructing him to wait by your side while you throw things, releasing him on his name or with *fetch* or *back*. But if your Labrador is a family clown, then there's nothing quite like the cliché

Catching a Frisbee is more of a skill than a trick, since it requires a dog to be coordinated enough to run under the flying disc, judge the distance, and leap to catch it.

of a Labrador chasing after and jumping to catch a Frisbee.

This is not really a trick; it is more a skill. Some dogs simply will not be coordinated enough to run under the flying disc, judge the distance, and leap to catch it. Some dogs, not the sharpest knives in the drawer, will chase the shadow and pounce on it, with the Frisbee hitting them in the head (which is also good for a laugh). Others just won't be able to put it all together. But if your dog displays some level of aptitude in catching and chasing things, he could be a candidate for catching a Frisbee.

You'll need some room to work on this skill, and you won't be able to wing it out there with all your strength at first. Rather, get the dog in front of you and just toss it to him. The pet stores now have soft cloth flying discs made especially for dogs; the hard plastic won't rap him in the teeth, and they're a bit easier for the dog to catch. Start moving farther back and toss the disc to the dog. Eventually, throw it slightly over his head and see if he goes and chases it. He may wait for it to come down at first; be patient. Soon he'll try to leap for it, provided you get his excitement level up. You should ultimately progress to the point where you can wing the disc at full force (giving it a bit of height to give the dog time to run under it) and watch your beast sail in the air and catch it. You'll be a hit at the city park.

ROLL OVER

Tricks are sometimes best taught with food rewards. They are commands you won't use all the time, so it's all right to give a treat whenever the dog pulls one off successfully. She may be a little hard of hearing in her excitement when you pull out the box of dog biscuits, but she'll soon understand that the box means a trick is required — no work, no pay. She may even begin rolling over at the mere sight of the treat box or the opening of the cupboard.

Teaching the *roll over* trick will require much manipulation on your part; you'll have to physically roll the dog over in order for there to be a reward. And the more excited you get, the more excited he'll get, which usually leads to a successful trick. The dog will learn the half-roll fairly quickly, rolling over onto his side and then back again without making a complete revolution. Don't reward the half-roller. Just keep pushing him all the way over and then give the reward.

You may want to get him into the *down* position first and then command, "Roll over!" You don't want him diving to the floor too hard in his excitement to get a treat. As you

Use a treat to make your dog roll over. At first, you'll probably have to push her through the full rotation.

push him along, command, "Roll over!" again, and when he's back on all fours, praise him lavishly and pay the Piper with a biscuit.

SHAKE I

This trick is very easy to teach, but it demands a gentle, even-tempered dog. The hyper dog may use this command as an opportunity to simply mob you. Make sure the pup holds his *sit* and *stay* positions efficiently before trying to teach *shake*.

This trick involves nothing more than gently taking the dog's paw and saying, "Shake," or, "Paw," or, "Gimmie five." Give the paw a few soft pumps, let it go, and toss him a bone. Don't use a food reward every single time, especially when just teaching the command, but you'll be surprised how quickly the food will open his ears.

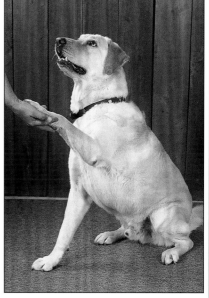

Getting your dog to shake is very easy—make sure you shake both paws!

After many repetitions, you should be able to just hold your hand out, and the dog will put his paw in yours. You can even say, "High five!" after he shakes, holding your hand up higher. And of course, we want these dogs to be ambidextrous, so make sure the pup gets a workout with both right and left paws. You can even use the commands, "Right," and, "Left," for the different paws.

SHAKE II

Also involving a "shake" but not in the paw sense, is teaching the dog to shake after getting out of the water. This is a very useful command for hunters — you can put the wet dog on the other end of the boat, away from you and the gear, and tell him, "Shake!" to make sure everything stays dry. To teach this, just anticipate when the dog will shake and give him the command. When the dog has progressed, you should be able to calmly accept a training bumper at heel from a wet dog, tell him, "Stay," walk away a few paces, and then order, "Shake."

This way, you'll be clear from the spraying water. If the dog doesn't quite get it at first, try holding his head between your hands just before he begins to shake. Dogs shake from the head back, so if his head can't move, he can't shake himself. Release his head and give the command.

BANG!

All of these tricks are party favors, of course, and one of the classics is *bang!* At first, you'll want to teach this to the dog while he's in the *down* position, but you should be able to do it while he's walking around as well. (By the way, if you think all guns are bad all the time, and you don't want to even pretend to shoot, my apologies for this one — but it *is* cute.)

With the pup lying down, command, "Bang!" Gently push him onto his side, and hold him there a few seconds. He'll need to be calm, and the dog that has mastered the *roll over* trick will think that he's supposed to flip all the way over. That's why you have to hold him there a few seconds. Repeat, "Bang!" while you're holding him, and then release him. After many repetitions, the pup should roll right onto his side and freeze when you "shoot" him with your finger.

The Bang! or playing dead trick is also great for reaffirming your dominance. A dog doesn't like to show his tender underbelly, and making him do so shows that you're in command.

With a lot of practice, your dog will learn how to flip the treat into the air and catch it before it hits the ground.

THE BONE ON THE SNOUT

Simply a classic. Every dog owner should try to teach this trick, if for no other reason than to teach a bit of canine patience. This will be a messy affair if the dog has a reputation for drooling at the sight of food, and some dogs will simply never get the hang of it. But, it's fun to watch them try.

You'll need the small size dog biscuits for this trick. Hold the dog's muzzle and place the bone crossways along the snout. Tell him, "Stay," and be firm about it. The dog will be a little cross-eyed at this point. You'll have to keep holding the muzzle at first. When he's held this pose for a few seconds, let him off the hook with an, "Okay!" or "Get it!" Dogs proficient at staying will remain frozen, or just drop their noses slowly until the biscuit falls off and onto the floor. But most dogs will learn to flip the biscuit in the air. The treat will fly around quite wildly at first, but soon the pup will develop a little finesse and toss it straight up and back down the hatch.

Keeping Your Dog Healthy

IF YOU WANT YOUR NEW BEST FRIEND TO LIVE A LONG and healthy life, then you must care about the simple things: appearance, hygiene, regular medical care, and physicals. And you mustn't choose this time to be frugal when it comes to veterinary bills. You owe it to the dog to give him the longest, healthiest life possible. This includes regular grooming and bathing, plenty of exercise, and keeping up on the shots. And the sooner you get the dog accustomed to a healthy lifestyle, the better his chances of fighting off diseases will be, and the easier it will be to keep him in tip-top shape.

PREVENTATIVE CARE

BATHING AND GROOMING

YOUR DOG IS GOING TO NEED to be bathed periodically. You don't want to over-bathe him, though, as this can lead to drying out of that wonderful water-resistant coat. And when you plan on bathing him, realize the fact that — unless you have some-place special like a laundry room with a big tub in it — your family bathroom will be a mess when you're finished and so will you. Labs do not need to be bathed often; their short coat lends itself to brushing quite nicely, and weekly brushings are much better than monthly bathings.

Simply washing the dog down with cool water will clean out much of the mud the dog may get into; in other words, you don't have to give him a full bath every time he gets a muddy paw. If he's just dusty, a good brushing is all he needs. But if he starts to smell like a dog, it's bath time. Before the bath, while the dog is still dry, thor-oughly brush him to remove any excess fur. Pick out a good shampoo that is formulated for dogs; don't use your shampoo on him — it will dry out his skin and fur. Follow the directions on the label as to how long to let it sit or how many lathers you have to do, but be fore-warned: You will probably need to rinse for a very long time to get all of the soap out. When you think it's gone, grab a fistful of fur and skin, and gently squeeze; you may see soapsuds form. If so, keep rinsing.

Comb and brush the dog once he settles down after the bath. Always let the bath be about good things; give him a treat afterwards if he was a good boy. He'll probably be a little hyper when he gets out and shakes off — he feels great! Let him outside, but not too long in the winter.

Cleaning the Ears

After a bath is also a good time to clean out his ears. Get an ear-cleaning solution from your veterinarian, and some cotton balls. Give a squirt down the ear canal, poke a cotton ball down the canal (be care-ful), and massage the dog's ear. Retrieve the cotton swab, and dab up any excess wax on the earflap. If you have questions, your veterinarian should be more than happy to give you a proper demonstration.

Cleaning the Teeth

You may also want to do something about his teeth on a regular basis. There are doggy toothpastes on the market, with poultry or beef flavors (he'll love them), and these can help to freshen his breath a bit, too. Don't use people toothpaste; the fluoride will upset his stomach. You should have been massaging the dog's gums since he was

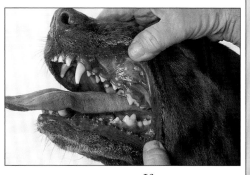

a puppy, so he should be used to having your fingers in his mouth. This pays dividends when it comes time to clean his teeth. Start with a swab and the toothpaste, and gently rub the teeth and gums; you can progress to a soft toothbrush if the dog will let you. Most often, he'll just try to bite it and think it's a game. The object here, really, is to get the toothpaste on the plaque. Enzymes in the toothpaste will break up the plaque without scrubbing.

If you massage your dog's gums starting when he is a puppy, he will be used to having your fingers in his mouth and won't struggle when it comes time for teeth care.

Dogs that hate to have their teeth cleaned may have to be put under to have them cleaned professionally by a veterinarian. Plaque buildup can lead to horrendous breath odor — just look at the food they eat! Giving the dog a crunchy carrot every now and then will help to scrape away some of the plaque and tartar, as do the toys that are designed to clean teeth. Indeed, it is hard to find a toy on the market that doesn't advertise its benefits for healthier teeth and gums. Some dogs will even let you scrape the plaque right off the teeth, but get instructions from a veterinarian if you plan to try this method. And if you have a dog like this, breed him or her! You'll have a waiting list for puppies.

Tooth diseases are not inherited, and this is one problem that can be completely preventable with careful attention from the owner. Gum disease can be an ugly mess and lead to tooth loss. Be sure to clean the dog's teeth regularly, and that means having the vet do it if you can't. Once a year, he should get a good cleaning; but if you can do it at home, you'll save on a hefty bill and give the dog healthier teeth and gums. Dog biscuits designed for teeth and gums will help, but they won't get all of the plaque and tartar off. If you notice a problem, jump on it. And don't just go by the canine teeth, the long pointed fangs you can readily see. Lift up his gums and check the molars in the back — that's where he crunches his food.

TRIMMING THE NAILS

Inspect his toenails. Clipping the nails will be one of the hardest things you'll do when grooming the dog; if you cut a nail back too far once and it bleeds, the dog will likely never let you near his feet again. It's better to be safe and cut less and more often than to go for a big cut. With yellow Labs, as you look at the nail from the side, see if you can see a pinkish center. This is where the blood supply is — don't cut it! Black and chocolate dogs have dark nails, so this handy reference point isn't visible. My black Lab and I have had some bloody encounters over nail clipping. Now, I just let the vet do it. For very young pups, your own nail clippers will work (turn them sideways when you're clipping because his nails are a different shape than yours). For older dogs, the clippers that look like a miniature guillotine work extremely well. A dog that has good feet — he runs on his toes — will most likely wear his nails down naturally with exercise.

IF THIS IS ALL TOO MUCH for you to handle, there are professionals who bathe and groom dogs. If you have any inclination of showing the dog in the ring, then you should consider a professional's help when it comes to styling up your Labrador, although most show-ring handlers are excellent groomers.

Above all, get the dog used to these experiences by starting them while he's young. One of the first things you should do when you bring the pup home is give him a bath, and you should constantly be gently touching his feet and mouth, never in a rough or playful manner. You don't want the adult dog to develop a phobia to the bathtub, nor do you want him suddenly snapping at you if you come near him when

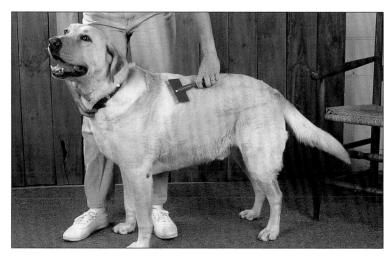

The key to grooming an adult dog is to start the experience when he's young.

it's time for a brushing or teeth cleaning. Socializing your puppy to these new situations will make for a more amenable adult. And nothing helps to prevent an older dog from developing nasty problems more than consistent attention from the moment you bring him home.

EXERCISE

ACTIVITY IS ONE OF THE MOST VALUABLE things for the health of a Labrador retriever. Your dog will require generous amounts of exercise throughout his lifetime, as has been stated and restated throughout this book. If he is going to be a hunting dog, then she should get plenty of work during the hunting season and training in the off season. However, if he is to be the family pet, you'll need to take extra measures to make sure he scratches that particular itch. And the benefit of having such a big dog that must be exercised is that it gets you out of the house as well.

Walks around the neighborhood are good to get the heart pumping, but you're going to have to let him stretch his legs, too. Find a city park, a mowed field, or a baseball diamond where the dog can run. Be sure to bring some plastic bags to pick up his donations to the health of the soil. Take training bumpers, a Frisbee, and other toys to get him to run, chase, and retrieve to keep him going. A play session with other dogs will also keep his legs pumping far longer than you'll be able to keep up.

One of the best forms of exercise, and one that is especially beneficial if he has any bone or joint problems or is an arthritic senior dog, is swimming. Let him swim back and forth, retrieving bumpers or a tennis ball.

Regular exercise will help control weight problems that may develop for the voracious eater, as well as keep the heart and lungs in shape.

It's best to choose a vet through recommendations from the breeder or other dog owners.

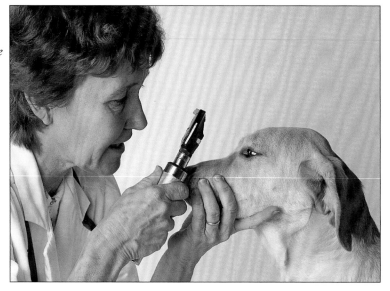

THE DOG DOC

IMMEDIATELY AFTER BRINGING THE PUPPY HOME, you should take him to see the veterinarian. The pup may be apprehensive at first with the strange smells and the office cat that insists on rubbing up against your leg. If you keep everything positive, you should have no problem

taking him back there for his regular checkups. But let's be realistic —
how positive can a rectal thermometer be?

Puppies will require several series of shots, spread out over the
course of their first four months of life. The breeder will probably give
him his first couple series, but you'll have to
make regular appointments to finish up.
These shots are vital, so don't wave them off
if they seem a bit pricey. In the last series,
your dog will get his annual rabies shot and
tag, and you'll probably get some heartworm medication for the summer months.

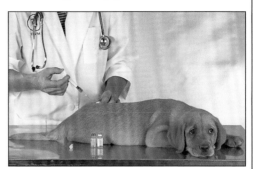

In selecting a veterinarian for your
Labrador, gather several recommendations
from other dog owners or the breeder. Your
business and your dog should be welcomed by the vet, and you should
be allowed to go into the exam room with your dog. If they don't want
you in back with the dog, either make it clear that the dog will behave
much better with you around, or find a new vet. You want to see everything that's done to your pooch.

Deadly or disabling diseases can easily be prevented with yearly vaccinations. Be sure to keep your dog up to date.

Your puppy probably won't need a heartworm test if he was born
in the winter months; you'll simply receive the beefy pills to start him
on. Take all heartworm tests and preventative medicine very seriously
— this is a life-threatening disease, and the shame of it is that it is
almost completely preventable. Heartworm tests are usually done
through a blood sample, right around the time you have the dog vac-
cinated for rabies (hookworm and pinworm are detected through stool
samples — remember that plastic bag?).

Your dog will also receive vaccinations against parvovirus and distemper, common canine diseases that were once life threatening. Now,
they are preventable with a vaccination that goes right along with the
rabies shot. There are other vaccinations as well to keep up to date:
Bordetella and lyme disease to name two. I won't go into the details of
how parvo, distemper, rabies, and heartworm manifest themselves.

You can get this information more completely from your veterinarian. This is not the place to discuss long-term health care for your dog; that place is in the office of a veterinarian you trust. Do make sure you stay current with your dog's shots because if you don't, disaster can strike.

FLEAS AND TICKS

ANOTHER HUGE THING you'll have to stay on top of is fleas and ticks. There are many pills and topical solutions that help to prevent both, either by keeping the bugs off the dog to begin with, or by killing the eggs. If your Lab is an outside or hunting dog, or if you are constantly around other dogs, you'll have to worry about fleas and ticks more. A thorough, regular brushing will help to spot problems should they crop up, and the quicker you notice them, the easier it will be to prevent a serious infestation.

Some of the topical solutions on the market do a wonderful job on ticks. These solutions, placed between the dog's shoulder blades where he can't lick at it, will leave the dog's fur greasy for a couple days, and with some brands, it's recommended that he not be wet for two days prior to and after application. But the dividends they pay in controlling fleas and ticks are worth the few days of no water training.

SPAYING AND NEUTERING

IF YOU DON'T PLAN to breed your Labrador retriever (and you should research the possibility thoroughly before even considering it), then it is wisest to have your male dog neutered and your female pup spayed. And the sooner the better. Ask your veterinarian as to when it is recommended they be "fixed," and try to make that appointment right away. For females, you'd like to get them spayed before their first heat cycle, right around five to six months of age. You'll have to cut out your training for a bit while they heal, but that won't be a problem. Males should be neutered as soon as possible.

Aside from helping to control their sex drives, fixing the dog also helps to reduce certain types of diseases, especially cancer. Females will be less likely to develop mammary cancer, while males will be less likely to develop testicular and prostate cancer. Fixing simply leads to an overall healthier lifestyle, as well as helping to control the pet population from accidental breedings. And no matter how well you think your dog is trained, when love is in the air, you'll be amazed at what the dog will do to get out and cruise the neighborhood. When it comes to spaying or neutering, my view is that it is both irresponsible and cruel *not* to fix a dog that will never be bred.

IF YOU STAY ON TOP OF PROBLEMS that develop, keep the dog's regular vaccination appointments, provide the necessary preventative medicine, and always contact your veterinarian when a question arises, there is no reason to think that your dog couldn't live to be 10 or 12, and perhaps several years beyond that (big dogs just don't live as long as little ones). Though it is a frighteningly short life span for such a cherished friend, you'll always remember the time you had with them. And the closer we get to them while they're alive, the longer they'll be with us when they're gone. Don't let the cost of medical care determine the lifespan of your dog.

LABRADOR RETRIEVER AILMENTS

BECAUSE YOU WANT YOUR DOG TO LIVE A LONG, HEALTHY LIFE, you must be aware of the typical problems experienced by Labrador retrievers, and dogs in general. If you go into the whole business of dog ownership with your eyes wide open, you'll be able to react responsibly and quickly when problems present themselves. And with such a hard-charging dog as a Lab, problems will present themselves.

All of the home remedies and anecdotal stories of how to cure canine illness pale beside the advice of a well-educated, trusted veterinarian. Whenever you have questions or think that a certain symptom might be the harbinger of something serious, take your dog to the vet. And though you may have a best friend who has had Labradors his whole life, don't put all of your trust in his home cures; trust the professionals 10 times out of 10.

ALLERGIES

Labradors are not especially prone to allergies, but some dogs are susceptible. Allergies can come from pollen, molds, dust mites, food, fleas, and other bugs. Allergies won't manifest themselves the same way in dogs as they do in humans. Instead of a stuffy nose, your dog will more than likely get scratchy skin.

Indeed, that is one of the best ways to spot the allergic dog: Look for the pooch that is constantly scratching, licking, or biting at his skin; a dull coat lacking texture or length; or, in some severe cases, a dog that is chewing on himself. These are clear signs that something's up, and you should seek the advice of a veterinarian. Be sure to ask your breeder about histories of allergies, and don't buy from the litter that has a pedigree of scratchy coats. Some allergies are in part hereditary.

Allergies that seem to occur seasonally may be caused by pollen or molds, and the dog's skin will be very itchy. Flea or other bug allergies will show up in the same manner. Food allergies will often present themselves as diarrhea, sneezing, ear problems, and in serious cases, seizures. Though food allergies are a bit more severe, they are easily treatable once you discover the food ingredient causing the reaction (just find a food without that item). If you suspect an allergy is plaguing your dog, consult with a veterinarian.

HOT SPOTS

Along the lines of allergies are "hot spots," or festering sores that spread rapidly from the dog constantly licking, biting, or scratching a particular spot. These can become quite serious, and it's surprising how quickly they can spread. A vet will show you the best methods for treating hot spots, and the beginning stages of treatment may even start at the veterinary clinic — in some cases, the dog will need to be sedated so the wound can be cleaned. The dog may even have to wear the dreaded "cone" (Elizabethan) collar to prevent him from digging back into the spot. There are many sprays and ointments available from your vet or the major pet supply companies that will help treat hot spots. Unfortunately, there is no real preventative measure for hot spots, as some dogs are just prone to them. But with careful attention to hygiene and grooming, you may reduce the dog's susceptibility.

Canine Hip Dysplasia (CHD)

This is a dreaded hip disorder that usually results in a painful, often shortened, lifespan for the dog. Sadly, because of the breed's popularity, a high percentage of Labs seem to be afflicted with this malady. It is a malformation of the hip ball-and-socket joint. Active sporting dogs are more prone to this disease, and Labradors fit the bill. This problem is almost entirely hereditary; that was why you checked for the Orthopedic Foundation for Animals (OFA) certification on your pup's mom and pop. Dogs with CHD should never be bred. A puppy is not born with CHD, how-

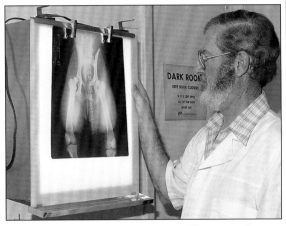

ever. You should have him x-rayed when he's about a year-and-a-half old to check his development, even if both his parents were OFA certified.

Have your dog screened for hip dysplasia when he's about 18 months old.

There are instances where OFA-certified parents can produce a puppy that, in the course of time, will develop symptoms of CHD. The dog leading a rough and tumble lifestyle, with lots of jumping and running on slick floors or concrete; the obese dog; and a dog on generous doses of calcium supplements can begin to show signs of the crippling disease. Symptoms are expressed in many ways, but moving both rear legs together in the characteristic "bunny hop," difficulty getting up from lying down or sitting, and low tolerance for having his rear legs and hip region touched are good indicators.

There is a new type of certification being used more often today. It is called the PennHIP method, and, unlike an x-ray, it measures a "distraction index" (DI) by compressing and then distracting the hip joint. It reads how far the head of the femur moves away from the socket; the result is a value between zero and one. There are averages for each breed, with, for example, a DI of .03 or lower indicating a dog negative for CHD. Dogs with values below this can be bred, and over the course of time, the DI will eventually get lower. Though OFA is still the standard certification — and much less expensive than the PennHIP method — you are likely to see both certifications for Labrador retriever parents from conscientious breeders.

Talk with your vet about possible treatments. These can range from expensive hip replacement surgeries in severe cases, to therapeutic exercise along with a daily pain reliever such as Rimadyl or Cosequin in less severe instances. A dog with CHD, however, can never lead the same active life as one without the malady.

SPORT-RELATED INJURIES

With such a hard-charging dog that is, for all practical purposes, a professional athlete, sport-related injuries are commonplace. However, with good — and common sense — conditioning during the off-season, you can keep those joints and muscles in good shape, preventing injuries that can otherwise occur by doing too much too fast.

There are some injuries that are not the fault of poor conditioning, however. Stepping in a hole while on a retrieve can lead to twisted or sprained ankles, or in serious cases, broken bones. The dog will have to go on the disabled list for a while; and, regrettably, with serious injuries, he may have to hang up his hunting shoes altogether. A torn ACL (anterior cruciate ligament) is a common sport-related injury, just as it is in humans. This ligament is roughly the same size in all dogs — a smaller cocker spaniel's ACL will be roughly the same size as the larger Labrador's, yet the Labrador will have more weight to support. Typically, an ACL blowout in Labradors is repaired with surgery and recovery in a soft cast for about six weeks, then slow rehabilitation. Some smaller breeds can heal with strict rest, but the big dogs almost always need surgery if the tear is complete. Several vets have told me that this injury is more prevalent among dogs that have been running in deep snow. If you live where the white stuff piles up, be careful.

EAR INFECTIONS

Because they seem to spend a lot of time in the water, your Lab will probably have problems with his ears sometime over the course of his life. Moisture trapped in the ear canal can lead to an infection — or at the least, a smelly ear — quite rapidly. As stated in the last chapter, every time you groom your dog, you should clean his ears.

The smell is a good first indication that there is a problem, along with his scratching and pawing at his ear, or pushing his head into your hands while you rub it. When you flip the ear over, you'll usually be greeted by a generous amount of wax. Follow the procedures outlined by your veterinarian for cleaning the dog's ears. You can obtain a good cleaning solution either from your vet or a pet supply company. Some solutions act as drying agents, evaporating quickly; all you have to do is squirt it down the canal.

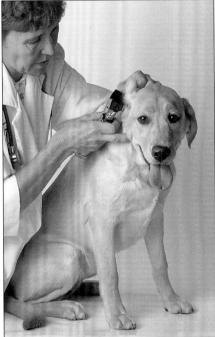

Spending a lot of time in water means ear trouble for many Labs.

With serious ear infections, the dog may have to be sedated so his ears can be cleaned; he can get a complete tune-up if you have his teeth cleaned at the same time. In severe cases, an ignored ear problem can lead to hearing loss later in life, so keep an eye on his ears.

OTHER CANINE PROBLEMS

THERE ARE NUMEROUS DISEASES that can afflict all dogs, and in particular those breeds that are large and active. It would be beyond the scope of this book to present every possible disease, their symptoms, and treatments; instead, I'll give a brief summary of some of the major things you can look for.

Inherited eye problems, especially *cataracts*, can afflict Labrador retrievers, even at a young age. It is important that the puppy's parents have a Canine Eye Registration Foundation (CERF) certification — the pup also can be certified at a fairly young age. Eye problems are relatively mysterious as to their cause. The clouding of the eyes of older dogs is a normal process of aging, but anything that looks serious probably is. Your best bet is to choose your breeder wisely — "picking the litter" is more important than "pick of the litter."

There are many *cancers* that can strike dogs during any age. Dogs can withstand chemotherapy better than humans, and that is one form of treatment if a malignant tumor is removed early. However, most dogs succumb to this terrible disease quickly, and the only option is to have the dog humanely put to sleep once the wrenching pain sets in.

Epilepsy is a baffling disease, manifesting itself in violent seizures at times, though some seizures may be nothing more than a period of time when the dog stares blankly and cannot be "snapped out of it." Some epileptic conditions are inherited, and some are brought on by the environment, other diseases, or a traumatic experience such as an accident. Be cautious of any head injuries your dog may sustain, and ask the breeder about her parents' history of seizures. Though it rarely causes the dog pain, seizures can be traumatizing for the owner to watch. In some cases, prescribed medication can help to control recurrences.

Thyroid problems, especially *hypothyroidism*, have been known to afflict Labrador retrievers. Dogs can be screened for thyroid abnormalities, and treatment can most often be in the form of a daily pill. Look for sudden weight gain, lethargy, and skin and coat problems (in particular, hair loss). This is usually not a life-threatening disease, but it should be looked at by a veterinarian as soon as possible.

You should also be sure that the prospective parents of your puppy have had their hearts checked out. There is some evidence that a new affliction is on the horizon for Labs: a heart problem known as *tricuspid valve dysplasia* (TVD). It is only detectible via an echocardiogram.

Your vet will check out your puppy's heart during the course of regular exams, but a stethescope won't uncover it; if you suspect any other problems, get the dog in immediately.

Limber tail or *cold tail*, as the latter name implies, seems to come from swimming in cold water. The dog can't lift his tail and he may bite at it. An inflammation

Make a dog first-aid kit. Items that should be included are:

■ *tweezers*	■ *hemostats*	■ *forceps*
■ *scissors*	■ *toenail clippers*	■ *thermometer*
■ *gauze pads*	■ *gauze roll*	■ *non-stick pads*
■ *adhesive tape*	■ *waterproof athletic tape*	
■ *eyewash*	■ *three-percent hydrogen peroxide*	
■ *earwash*	■ *Nolvasan (wound cleanser)*	
■ *Calamine lotion*	■ *antibiotic ointment*	
■ *Pepto-Bismol*	■ *Bufferin (no Advil or Ibuprofen)*	

Ask your veterinarian for further help in assembling a doggy first-aid kit, and be sure to pack it away in the car or with your hunting/camping gear. You will find that much of the same stuff that works on humans will also work on dogs.

of the glands at the base of the tail is the culprit. The condition normally resolves itself in a few days.

In all cases, a watchful eye can either prevent diseases or prevent them from becoming serious. The dog can't tell you where it hurts, but his actions can tell you that it does. You'll have to accept responsibility for providing the necessary medical attention when it warrants. As mentioned repeatedly, nothing replaces the advice of a trusted veterinarian. And most will let you call in with a question every now and then, without bringing the dog in for a full visit.

Hunting Retriever Training

THIS SECTION WILL GIVE AN OVERVIEW OF THE SKILLS necessary for your Labrador retriever to begin upland and waterfowl hunting. It does not cover everything, as hunting and field trialing constantly demand new skills of the dog. To hunt with your dog, you'll find the pursuit is full of surprises, and thus, it is only feasible to prepare your dog for what he will most likely encounter. With these basic skills, in addition to a mastery of the four basic commands described in a previous chapter, you should have a dog that will be well on its way to being a valuable hunting companion.

EQUIPMENT

THE FOLLOWING TEXT outlines the necessary equipment you'll need to teach your pup the basics of upland and water-fowl hunting. These can be bought at a quality hunting store or dog specialty catalog company; just about all of their products will stand the rigors of the field and water.

EQUIPMENT FOR HUNTING TRAINING

BASIC:

- hunting collar (usually orange for the uplands)
- 20- to 50-foot checkcord
- blank pistol
- whistle
- retrieving bumpers
- artificial scent
- a few pen-raised birds

ADVANCED:

- dummy launcher
- bird launcher or "winger"

SOME HUNTING TERMINOLOGY

YOU SHOULD BE FAMILIAR WITH SOME basic hunting and dog-handling terms:

A MARK refers to a bird (or training bumper) that the dog sees fall; he "marked" its location.

A BLIND is one that he did not see fall.

Pointing the dog in the direction of the object to be retrieved and having him run straight to it is called a LINE.

Directing a dog to a mark or a blind by giving him directions while he's out searching for the object is called HANDLING.

Obviously, one object to retrieve is called a SINGLE; two objects equal a DOUBLE (even though they are always properly retrieved one at a time), and so forth.

To FORCE-FETCH a dog means that the dog will fetch any object on command as a result of a training process, not just natural instinct; this is a vital training exercise that ensures the dog will retrieve and hold the bird until you issue the command to give instead of dropping it at your feet.

There are many types of retrieving bumpers on the market, and it's hard to go wrong in picking any of the brands. However, stick to white bumpers for young dogs, and use the fluorescent orange ones during more advanced training. Dogs are virtually blind to that color, so these bumpers will work well when you train on blind retrieves. Attaching a streamer to the bumper will allow the dog to better follow a thrown mark. The small protuberances on some bumpers will help the dog develop a soft mouth. Also, the retrieving bumpers in the shapes of ducks, geese, or pheasants add a realistic feel and weight in the dog's mouth, and the loose head helps to dissuade the dog from shaking the object.

STEADINESS refers to the act of the dog sitting still next to you while you are either hunting or throwing a mark for him to retrieve. The dog that is truly steady will not break with any distractions, and will only go when you give him the command.

WATERFOWL HUNTING

IN WATERFOWL HUNTING, you need the dog to bring the bird back to you. When you were teaching the four basic commands, you should have practiced putting them all together: from sitting the dog out in front, telling him to *come* and then *heel*, and then to *sit* once he was at your side. This is the finishing position for the dog, and it should be one of only two positions from which you accept the bird, the other being in front — the *front finish* position.

If you have played fetching games with your pup enough, you should have confidence in his ability and instinct to retrieve. Now it's time to get more formal. Start in a mowed lawn with bright white bumpers (they are easy for the dog to see) and place a few drops of artificial scent on the bumper to get him excited. With the pup at your side, toss the bumper and let him chase it down. At first, you want to keep everything fun and interesting. If he seems overly intense, be thankful — you can always tone it down a bit, but you can't put drive into the dog. Physically restrain him a bit longer each time, then send him on the retrieve, saying his name each time he leaps from your hands. This is an old handler's technique — use the dog's name to

Use bright white bumpers when you begin retriever training, as they are easy for the pup to see.

send him when he can see the object to be retrieved — a *mark*. Use the *back* command to send him for an object he cannot see — a *blind*. You may want the checkcord on him at this point to make sure he comes back to you; once he gets the bumper in his mouth, he may want to run off with it. Instead, just reel him in with the checkcord, and praise him when he delivers the bumper (even if you have to tickle his tongue to get it). Don't get carried away with praise, however; a simple "Good, Roscoe" is enough. Above all, you want to be sure he comes back to you at this point in his training. You have to instill the fact that if he brings it back, you'll keep throwing it.

When he gets a bit older and is efficient in the simple, playful retrieves, then you can start formal training. With the pup at heel, command, "Stay," and throw the bumper. Have a tight hold on the checkcord at first, and be ready for him to lunge. Just command, "Stay," again. Place your hand over the dog's head, karate-chop fashion, lining it right toward the mark. Say his name in an excited voice, and release the checkcord. He should bound away with pent-up excitement. When he pounces on the bumper, command, "Come," and remind him with a few tugs on the checkcord. As he gets nearer, command him to the *heel* position, and have him *sit* to finish.

Now at this point, because the pup has not been force-fetched, he will probably drop the bumper when he gets close to you. Though you'll never fully stop this until you force-fetch him, you can get him used to bringing it all the way to you by moving backward as he comes near. When he gets close, step forward quickly, and scoop it from his mouth, commanding, "Give." Praise him for his first marked retrieve.

For the next couple weeks, you should work extensively on these

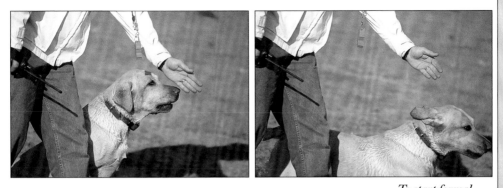

single marks, making sure he stays at heel until you give him the order to go. The more you stress steadiness, the more it will help him to stay in the duck blind with you instead of busting loose at every shot. He may start to bring the bumper all the way to you before dropping it, which will help come force-fetching time. You can throw in some double marks here and there, but don't expect any glowing performances. Have a helper stand about 20 yards away and throw the bumper. The pup should watch intently, mark the retrieve, and bring it back to you — not the thrower. If he starts to move toward the thrower, the thrower should ignore him; a checkcord is vital here to get him to come back to you. This helps to get the point across that not all retrieves come from your hand — some are "out there," too.

To start formal retriever training, command, "Stay," and throw the bumper. Place your hand over the dog's head, karate-chop fashion, lining it right toward the mark. Send the dog on his name.

LINING

YOU SHOULD ALSO BE WORKING on his lining skills. To do this, place the pup on *stay*, and drop a series of bumpers in a line in front of him, ranging from five to 30 yards. Line him toward the bumpers, and send him. When he picks the closest one up and brings it back, line him up again, and send him to the next one in line until he has retrieved all of the bumpers. This will not only teach him lining skills, but it will develop his range on the marks. If doing this in the wintertime, try shoveling out a path in the snow to help the dog run straight toward the bumpers. If you have access to a trail or a walking path, these are great for this drill, influencing the dog to stay on line as he heads for a retrieve. Incidentally, staying on line going and coming during a retrieve is not just stylish, it's safe. A dog that safely traverses a field or negotiates water to get to a downed bird gets in less trouble and danger if he returns by the same route. You can choose his route when he goes out; but if he returns by a different path, he can get hung up, step into a hole on a dead run, or come in contact with a dangerous obstacle.

HANDLING

AFTER SEVERAL WEEKS of this type of training, the pup will be proficient at marks and lining, delivering the bumper to heel (or at least himself to heel), and he will have had exposure to multiple retrieves. Now is the time to start working on his handling skills. Handling a dog is seen most on blind retrieves, where the dog does not see the object fall. But it is also an essential tool if, for instance, you have two ducks down on the water, one is dead and one is crippled. You can call the dog off the easy retrieve and direct him toward the cripple before it gets away. Teaching the concept of handling is best done with an exercise called the "baseball drill."

Imagine your yard is the infield on a baseball diamond. *Sit* and *stay* the dog at the pitcher's mound, and walk away from him about five yards to home plate. With him still at *stay* (and you need some dog control here because of his excitement), toss a single mark toward first base. He may turn his body to face the bumper — that's all right at this point. Get his attention back to you, though, with a couple tugs on the checkcord. When he is looking at you, over-exaggerate a pointing gesture with your entire arm toward first base while you say, "Over." The pup may not go at first because you've been sending him on his name; just keep saying, "Over," and use body language to get him to go. When he does go and brings the mark back to heel, pour on the praise — the pup has just been handled to his first mark.

Keep repeating these simple *overs* to first and third base, walking him back to the pitcher's mound each time after he delivers the bumper. Next, toss one over his head toward second base. He will probably break to run after it, so don't be discouraged. Just bring him back and put him at the pitcher's mound again facing you at the home plate position. He may completely turn his body around to see the bumper, and you may have to go out and straighten him up so he's facing you again. Get his attention on you, and command an enthusiastic, "Back!" while you shoot your hand straight up. The dog should perfectly wheel around and race toward the bumper, but he probably won't at first. It will take many repetitions for him to follow *back* correctly, but it is one of the most essential skills in hunting. *Back* will keep the dog going after the bird if it is swimming away, or if the dog loses sight of it or becomes disoriented and comes up short.

If you plan on hunting your Labrador retriever or campaigning him in field trials, you should visit the Bird Dog Foundation in Grand Junction, Tennessee. Located there is the Retriever Field Trial Hall of Fame, featuring some of the most famous Labs to ever play the game.

Over the course of the next week or so, you should be able to throw multiple marks to multiple bases, and the pup should be able to be sent to whichever one you direct him to. For example, you should be able to sit him at the mound, go to home plate, and toss a bumper to each base and send him to make the retrieve you indicate.

If he has been trained with the whistle as well, be sure to incorporate the whistle with any spoken commands, in particular *sit* and *come*. This will allow you to stop the dog with a single whistle blast while he is out searching for the bumper, or when he heads for the wrong mark. You will then be able to give him a direction toward it. But be careful not to overdo it, or the dog won't go out in the first place; he'll stop the second he can't find the bird and look at you for directions. This is a fault called *popping*, in which the dog stops displaying initiative and looks to you for reinforcement or direction every step of the way, and it's completely handler induced.

Once he can be handled toward marks, start laying blind retrieves for him. Without him looking (and you may have to leave him in the house while you hide the bumpers), stash a couple of bumpers in some not-too-obvious places. Bring him out, line him up, and send him. The pup might run out a bit confused at first and look back at you for a direction. Use your judgment as to whether you feel you should give him a *back* or just ignore him and let him go. When he gets in the vicinity of the bumper, he should smell it (if you've scented it, and probably even if you haven't). If he's been running a straight line, he should run right in to it. If he gets lost, stop him and handle him toward it.

Preparing for the Real Deal

To prepare your Lab for actual waterfowl hunting, while working on simple marks right through to blinds, scatter some decoys on the lawn and have the pup work through them. Walk him at heel around them and tell him, "No," if he starts to pick one up. Get him used to seeing them while he's going for the mark, and have him run right through a spread to retrieve a bumper.

It is also imperative that the dog gets used to the duck call and the gun. Incorporate the blank pistol whenever you throw marks for him (or most times), and even toot on the duck call a bit before throwing the mark and firing the gun. You can have a helper do all of this as well, so you can concentrate on the dog. Have the helper fire the blank pistol and throw the mark, gradually moving closer until you are firing the pistol and eventually shotgun blanks while the helper throws the mark. Gun-shyness is most often an inherited trait, but gun "nervousness" is another handler-induced fault — too much loud shooting, too close, too soon.

When out in the duck marsh, it's a good idea to carry a pair of white gloves with you. You'll be donned in your camouflage, and the dog may have a hard time picking you out against the background when you need to give him a hand signal. A flashing white glove will grab his attention.

A dummy launcher is a powerful device that will shoot a retrieving bumper much farther than you can throw one, and it incorporates the sound of the gun as well. Plus, it gets the dog past the *static distance* — the distance he knows you can throw a bumper. If you can throw one 30 yards, his experience tells him not to bother looking beyond that distance if he loses track of the mark. The launcher lets him see that there is not a "set distance" for a mark to be thrown. Make sure your dog can perform long retrieves before using one, however.

One of the most important things the pup must do is come when called. You must be able to give him whistle signals to stop him, get his attention away from a bird, and call him back to you. This is important in the case of a crippled duck getting away from the dog. You have to be able to call the dog back so you can dispatch the cripple, and then send the dog for the retrieve. Use the checkcord to teach this skill, but don't overdo it. If done too often, the dog will simply refuse to go because he'll think he's just going to be called in.

The final step in preparing the dog for his first waterfowl hunting is to move your drills — marks, blinds, simple handling — to the water. Get the dog used to obeying the commands in the waves as well as he did in the grass. You will find you'll be able to train a lot longer in the water, but dogs do get hot even when swimming. Don't wear him out com-

After your dog has mastered retrieving on dry land, you must move your drills to the water so he'll be ready for the hunting environment.

pletely. If you plan to hunt out of a boat, practice sending him from the boat while it's on shore so you don't have to worry about tipping over. You can also teach him that there's a particular spot for him to sit, preferably near a dog ladder that will help him get into the boat.

UPLAND HUNTING

UPLAND HUNTING IS DIFFERENT from waterfowl hunting in one fundamental way: In the uplands, the dog is out in front of you seeking game instead of sitting next to you waiting for you to shoot. Therefore, it is imperative that you establish the dog's confidence of being out ahead, in the lead, and using his nose to find game.

You can start this when the pup is very young when you take him out in the yard to play. Wherever he runs, turn so that he is in front of you. If he runs past you, turn and face him, walking after him. Throw in the command, "Hunt 'em up!" to get him to understand that he needs to be out in front. Although they are a breed with a lot of drive, some Labradors may want to hang by your side, especially if you've been insistent when teaching the *heel* command. It will take some coaxing to get the message across that it is now okay for him to run ahead, and the pup may shy away from it at first. There is good reason for the confusion. You have been working very hard on obedience and sitting and staying. Now, you seemingly are abandoning all of that and asking the dog to (from his point of view) run around mindlessly with no set task to be performed. It is a tribute to the Lab's intelligence and breeding that he or she is able to sort out the difference and perform both hunting regimens well. You'll find that your dog may come to favor one type of hunting over the other. My own Lab, Roxie, being on the hyper side, much prefers a pheasant field to a duck blind because she does not have to sit still — in fact, sitting still is the last thing either of us wants her to do. In a duck blind when the action is slow, she starts to fidget and usually ends up eating my lunch when I'm not looking.

So keep encouraging him to go ahead. Wave your hand in front as you say, "Hunt 'em up!" and let him explore. The best place to do this is not in your lawn but in a field of some sort, where the dog's natural curiosity will get the better of him, and he'll have to explore.

Once the dog is proficient at staying ahead, you'll have to keep him in range. A retriever that flushes game out of shotgun range (beyond 40 yards) is about worthless, so you have to teach the pup that there is a boundary to how far he can explore, both in front of you and to the sides. The best way to do this is with a 20- to 50-foot checkcord.

Though you may incorporate a command to tell the dog to stay closer —usually whistling to him or blowing the *whistle-sit* command to get him to sit and face you when he gets too far out — will indicate that you want him to move closer. As the dog matures, he'll learn the point at which he can go before you start hollering at him, and he'll naturally start to limit himself to that distance. But the trick you want the pup to master is the art of *quartering* a field.

With the checkcord attached to his collar, keep up behind him (you'll have to run at first — you don't want the dog to walk while he's hunting), and let him run ahead. When he gets to the end of the checkcord, let him tug on it, and say, "Closer," or some other command you may want to use to keep him in a bit.

To get him to run from one side to the other, you'll have to show him how to do it. When the pup is out front, get his attention and say, "This way," holding up your hand to the side, almost like you're giving the *over* command. Start jogging or walking in that direction, giving a slight tug on the leash also in that direction. He should naturally begin to follow your lead, though he'll still be out front 20 to 35 yards. Once he runs in that direction for about 30 yards, get his attention again and say, "This way," while you hold up your other hand, now running in the opposite direction, laying down a zigzag course. He again should follow. While you're doing this, be sure to keep going forward.

It's a great pleasure to watch an experienced dog go after a retrieve.

Once the pup is confident out in the lead, and he starts to get the hang of running from one side to the other, you can let go of the checkcord, and you won't have to keep walking in your zigzag pattern. Simply whistle to him and tell him, "This way," in whatever direction you hold up your hand. Soon, he'll learn the side boundaries he can go before he is whistled to turn back and run the other way. And sooner than you think, you won't need to whistle at all when it comes time to turn.

It is really something to watch an experienced dog work the wind, quartering a field so as to put the most scent in front of his nose.

Though there are advanced training methods that help to reinforce this natural hunting instinct, they are too detailed for this book. But a small drill to help with the quartering skill is to place pen-raised, dizzied pigeons or quail at the extreme right and left sides of the pup's quartering pattern, with the next bird approximately 30 to 50 yards ahead of the previous bird. He'll get the hang of racing from one side of the field to find a bird, then to the other to find the next one. Once in the wild, he'll use this quartering pattern to locate game.

You should incorporate a blank pistol whenever you're doing something fun and interesting with the dog. You introduced the pup to loud noises at mealtime when he was a puppy, you moved up to louder noises while he was play retrieving, and he got a thorough introduction in his waterfowl training, right up to blanks fired in a shotgun. Now should be the time to use the blank pistol while letting him romp in the field and retrieve thrown bumpers. So, whenever you throw a bumper for the pup or he flushes a bird, fire the pistol. You want him to experience nothing but pleasure when that sound goes off; otherwise you may have a gun-shy dog. And a gun-shy hunting dog is about as useful as the instructions on how to fill out your 1040 tax form.

PREPARING FOR HUNTING

IF THE PUP IS TO BECOME a good bird dog, he's going to need birds. Nothing is more valuable to a hunting dog than real experience with birds. These may be pen-raised pigeons or quail, farm ducks or pheasant, and they can be in bird launchers or simply spun and dizzied. They can have their flight feathers clipped so they'll run and leave a scent trail for the pup to track, or you can leave them as fliers, so you can shoot the bird and let the dog fetch the downed game. Whatever combination you choose — and you should escalate from a flight-clipped bird, to dizzied birds, to as much of a real hunting situation as you can manage — be sure to give the dog lots of exposure. You

Get the pup acquainted with feeling feathers in his mouth early on with wings, tails, or dead birds.

already should have been exposing him to birds since puppyhood — with wings, tails, or dead birds — so he should be used to the sensation of feathers in his mouth.

USING A WHISTLE IN UPLAND HUNTING

A WHISTLE IS AN ESSENTIAL COMPONENT of a hunter's gear. It will get through to the dog in windy conditions when your voice cannot, and often a dog will obey a whistle command much faster than a spoken command. If you've been training the pup on various whistle commands during the four basic command training sessions (in particular, *sit* and *come*), the pup has learned to recognize it as another form of instruction. Now, you'll use the whistle mainly to get his attention. When he stops to look at you, you can see where he is, turn him in a different direction, or get him to follow a command.

However, don't get into the habit of using the whistle too much too early. You want the pup to develop confidence on his own, so don't overly correct him. It will take some time for him to slide into his own in the field; but if you've constantly insisted upon blind obedience, he won't trust his nose to find game — he'll think you'll always put him onto birds. The job of the dog is to find game for us.

When you get to the point where you want to start shooting birds over the pup, it helps to have an assistant do the shooting. You want to concentrate on the dog. If the pup has been efficient in bringing the game back to heel, which you should have had him doing during his waterfowl training, then he'll be ready for the commands and will bring the game in the uplands back to your side. Be sure not to allow the pup to scamper off with the bird or lie down and chew it; you need the dog to softly deliver the bird to your hand. Praise him lavishly, and send him again with a, "Hunt 'em up!"

There is no better training for the uplands than going upland hunting. There is a great deal of truth to the notion that the birds will teach the dogs; your job is to take the dog out hunting. If he has mastered the basic commands, will take your directions to multiple birds and blinds, and will deliver things to you consistently, then experience and bird contact will finish him in style.

FORCE-FETCHING

FORCE-FETCHING, OR FORCE-BREAKING, is an exercise involving pressure that is used to teach the dog to *fetch, hold,* and *give* on command. It should be done when the dog's adult teeth have come in, around six to eight months of age. Warning: This can be an unpleasant procedure to teach your dog, and if you have any questions, consult a professional trainer. Some dogs will pick up on it right away; others will take weeks. Whatever you do, take your time and quit all other training until the skill is learned.

You first need to teach the dog the *hold* command. Get him up on top of his kennel or a table (to save your back), and have him sit and

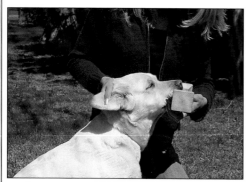

In force-fetching, the first command to teach is hold.

stay. The pup must be able to stay efficiently so he won't run away from the pressure. Pry his mouth open by grasping the top of his snout and inserting your fingers behind his canine teeth. When he opens his mouth, insert the bumper, and close his mouth shut. Command, "Hold." He will struggle at first, and he may even paw at you. Don't squeeze his mouth shut, but gently hold it around the bumper. When he begins to hold the bumper a little longer on his own, put your finger in the V under his chin, and push upward, pushing his head up. This will help him to keep his mouth closed.

Whenever you take the bumper from the dog, command, "Give." Pause a few seconds between the *hold* and *give* commands so that the pup does not get confused. When you've progressed over the course of several days, you should be able to try to pull the bumper out of his mouth; he should hold onto it until you say, "Give."

When the pup will hold a variety of objects without assistance, move on to the *fetch* command. It may seem odd to say you're teach-ing the dog to fetch when he already has displayed great enthusiasm for doing just that. But in *forcing* the dog to fetch, you can get the pup to pick up anything you want him to and *hold* it until you tell him to release it to you. This will create a dog that will *fetch* every single object, *hold* it all the way back to the *heel* position, and *give* it on your command.

Hold the bumper in front of his nose. Pinch his ear flap until he starts to complain, and when he opens his mouth, stick the bumper in at the same time you release the pressure on his ear. Once it's in his mouth, command, "Hold," and pet him while he sits there. Tell him how wonderful he is, pet his feet and lift them up, or walk away. Command, "Give," when you're ready to take the bumper back. Do not say, "Fetch," at this point; you want the pup to understand that the ear pinch means *fetch*. You are telling him that the discomfort will stop when he has the bumper in his mouth. He will quickly learn to reach for the bumper when you reach for his ear, which is precisely what you want.

Start to incorporate, "Fetch," just after you pinch his ear. It is the same way you taught the *whistle-sit* command — you said, "Sit," something the dog knew the meaning of, then gave the whistle. Over time, you phased out the spoken command. Here, the dog knows what the ear pinch means, then you give the spoken command. Soon, you can phase out the ear pinch. He should reach for and take anything you hold up for him on the command, "Fetch."

Move the object to be retrieved farther from his face and toward the floor. Evolve to the point where you can place it on the floor with a couple of fingers on it to indicate that it is the object to be retrieved. If the pup falters at all when you give him the *fetch* command, move in quickly with an ear pinch to remind him, repeating, "Fetch." This is not the place for discipline or a bad temper — you have to remain calm to keep the dog calm. After a week or two, the pup will be able to fetch anything you indicate on command, and hold it until you have given him the order to release.

RESOURCES

THERE ARE MANY DRILLS and exercises you can do to hone the skills of your hunting Labrador, and you may even desire to enter the dog in various field trials or hunt tests. For more advanced training techniques, there are a number of professional trainers you can seek out, and some offer open clinics.

The list of resources of books, videos, magazines, professional trainers, and hunting buddies who have trained dogs is endless. Some of the more renowned trainers who have published books on retriever training include: Richard Wolters, Bill Tarrant, James Lamb Free, D.L. Walters, and Jim and Phyllis Dobbs. You should consult these sources for a complete guide to producing a crackerjack retriever.

IN ADDITION TO THE RESOURCES LISTED BELOW, there are numerous Labrador retriever sites on the Internet via any search engine. There are also many state and local clubs and organizations.

Don't rule out the possibility of obtaining your Labrador retriever from a "rescue" dog organization, those clubs or groups that rescue lost or abandoned dogs, or those from irresponsible breeders. These rescued dogs are usually adults, so any problems that would not have been evident in a puppy have already been identified and/or remedied.

AWARDS AND CERTIFICATES

FOLLOWING IS A LIST OF AWARDS and certificates a Labrador retriever can earn in competition, both in the field via hunt tests or field trials, or in the show-ring. The designations by the following organizations are helpful to know when examining the pedigree of a puppy prior to purchase.

AMERICAN KENNEL CLUB (AKC)

The American Kennel Club has many events in which titles are offered. Dogs that achieve these are entitled to have them listed on their pedigrees and certificates and in event catalogues. These titles become an official part of a dog's record. Listed below are the various official AKC titles with their abbreviations:

As a prefix:

CH   Champion (conformation)
FC   Field Champion
AFC   Amateur Field Champion
NFC   National Field Champion
NAFC   National Amateur Field Champion

NORTH AMERICAN HUNTING RETRIEVER ASSOCIATION (NAHRA)

■ A STARTED RETRIEVER (SR) CERTIFICATE is awarded to a dog that earns 10 points (4 qualifications @ 2.5 points each) in the STARTED testing category.

■ A WORKING RETRIEVER (WR) CERTIFICATE is awarded to a dog that earns 20 points (4 qualifications @ 5 points each) in the INTERMEDIATE testing category.

■ A MASTER HUNTING RETRIEVER (MHR) CERTIFICATE is awarded to a dog that earns either:
    ■ 100 points (5 qualifications @ 20 points each) in the SENIOR testing category, or . . .
    ■ 80 points (4 qualifications @ 20 points each) in the SENIOR testing category and already has a WORKING RETRIEVER title.

■ A GRAND MASTER HUNTING RETRIEVER (GMHR) CERTIFICATE is awarded to a dog that earns 300 points (15 qualifications @ 20 points each) in the SENIOR testing category.

■ TITLE CERTIFICATES are awarded on the completion of category point requirements and the submission of the dog's registration (copy) to NAHRA Headquarters. Office: 540/286-0625 Fax: 540/286-0629. NAHRA titles are placed before the dog's name.

■ BRASS BAND/ REGIONAL INVITATIONAL FIELD TEST. A dog that qualifies in either 4 STARTED or 4 INTERMEDIATE tests within a calendar year (Jan. 1 to Dec. 31) will receive a Brass Band Award. The dog will also be qualified to participate in a Started/Intermediate Regional Invitational Field Test held in the following calendar year.

UNITED KENNEL CLUB/HUNTING RETRIEVER CLUB (UKC/HRC)

HRC is affiliated with the United Kennel Club, Inc., Kalamazoo, MI, which carries the registry for the HRC. The UKC offers 4 titles to the HRC program: HUNTING RETRIEVER (HR); HUNTING RETRIEVER CHAMPION (HRCH); GRAND HUNTING RETRIEVER CHAMPION (GRHRCH); and UPLAND HUNTER (UH). In addition, a movement is underway to create a STARTED RETRIEVER (SR) title for the HRC Hunt Test program. In keeping with the philosophy of HRC, titles earned are awarded as a prefix to the dog's name on its pedigree, as opposed to a suffix to the name. The United Kennel Club, Inc., established in 1898, is the second largest all-breed dog registry in the U.S., registers over 250,000 dogs each year, and licenses 10,000 challenging, fun, relaxed, family-oriented events annually.

CLUBS AND ORGANIZATIONS

AMERICAN KENNEL CLUB
5580 Centerview Dr.
Raleigh, NC 27606
(919) 233-9767
www.akc.org

CANINE EYE REGISTRATION FOUNDATION
   (CERF)
1248 Lynn Hall
Purdue University
West Lafayette, IN 47907
(317) 494-8179
vet.purdue.edu/depts/prog/cerf.html

ORTHOPEDIC FOUNDATION FOR ANIMALS
   (OFA)
2300 Nifong Blvd.
Columbia, MO 65201
www.offa.org

SYNBIOTICS (PENNHIP)
11011 Via Frontera
San Diego, CA 92127

NORTH AMERICAN HUNTING RETRIEVER
   ASSOCIATION
P.O. Box 6
Garrisonville, VA 22463
(703) 752-4000
www.nahra.org

BIRD DOG FOUNDATION
P.O. Box 774
505 W. Highway 57
Grand Junction, TN 38039
(901) 764-2058
www.fielddog.com

OTHER INTERNET SITES OF
INTEREST:
WORKING RETRIEVER CENTRAL:
   www.working-retriever.com
NATIONAL EDUCATION FOR ASSISTANCE DOG
   SERVICES: www.neads.org
THE RETRIEVER JOURNAL:
   www.villagepress.com/wildwood/rj2.html